7 STEPS TO GET OUT OF DEBT AND BUILD WEALTH

Library and Archives Canada Cataloguing in Publication

Omole, Adeola

7 Steps to Get Out of Debt and Build Wealth: How I Paid off Over $390,000 of Debt and Built a 7-Figure Net Worth By Implementing The Supercharged Financial Strategy

ISBN 978-1-7752344-0-1 (paperback)
ISBN 978-1-7752344-1-8 (ebook)

1. Finance, Personal. I Title.

Edited by Marnie Ferguson
Book design and production by WeMakeBooks.ca

The following information is intended as a general reference guide for understanding the underlying principles and practices of the subject matter covered, and should not be viewed as the ultimate source for financial information. It is sold with the understanding that neither the author nor publisher are engaged in rendering legal, accounting, financial, or other professional services by publishing this book. Since each individual situation is unique, questions pertaining to personal finances and financial advice should be addressed to an appropriate financial professional to ensure that the individual gets personalized financial advice that has been evaluated carefully and appropriately, and that is specific to the individual's unique situation. The author and publisher assume no responsibility for errors or omissions and expressly disclaim any responsibility for any liability, loss, or risk which is incurred as a consequence, directly or indirectly, of the use and application of any of the contents of this book.

Published in Canada

Published By: Millenium Asset Management Corp
PO Box 27027 Tuscany
Calgary, Alberta T3L 2Y1
Canada
Toll Free: 1-800-348-9788
E-mail: customerservice@adeolaomole.com
Website: www.adeolaomole.com
Facebook: @adeolaomolefan
Twitter: @AdeolaOmoleB
Instagram: @adeolaomoleb

If you are interested in bulk orders of *7 Steps to Get Out of Debt and Build Wealth*, we offer an aggressive discount schedule. Please call the above number for more details.

Printed in Canada

Printed on 100% post-consumer recycled paper

7 STEPS to Get Out of DEBT and Build WEALTH

How I Paid Off Over $390,000 of Debt and Built a 7-Figure Net Worth by Implementing the *Supercharged Financial Strategy*

ADEOLA OMOLE

SUPERCHARGE. YOUR. LIFE.

MILLENIUM ASSET
MANAGEMENT CORP

To Adam—my husband and best friend,
thank you for your unwavering support.
I am so grateful for you.
To my kids—Aidan and Alina,
thank you for your unconditional love.
The two of you are the best gifts in the world.
I love you all so much!

Table of Contents

INTRODUCTION

**I don't ever want to depend
on the kindness of banks.**

−BEN GRAHAM

Fifteen years ago I had over $70,000 of consumer debt, not including my mortgage. At the time I was young, broke and scared, and I did not think it was possible to get out from under my huge pile of debt. I had just completed writing my bar exams and was excited about my bright future as a new lawyer. However, I was terrified about the massive pile of debt that was looming over me. A sudden job loss resulted in my being out of work for eighteen months and forced me to face my debt head on. My financial situation was dire as I had been living paycheque to paycheque, had no financial safety net, and had a negative net worth.

Not knowing where to turn, I decided to learn everything I could about personal finance, money management, debt repayment strategies, and investing. After reading hundreds of books I developed my own debt repayment and wealth creation strategies. I have written this book so I can share how I was able to get out of over $70,000 of consumer debt in less than three years, how I paid off over $320,000 owed on my home in twelve years and how I turned my debt repayment strategy into an opportunity to create wealth.

The most important financial decision that I ever made was to get out of debt. Once I made that decision my life changed for the better. I was able to stand in my truth and live my life authentically because I no longer had the burden and stress that come with having debt. If you are drowning in debt, please rest assured that there is a way out and I am going to show you how.

I'm very excited to share my **Supercharged Financial Strategy**. It is the combination of two powerful plans: **Supercharged Debt Repayment Plan (SDRP)** and **Supercharged Wealth Accumulation Plan (SWAP)**. Also, I can't wait for you to share what you've learned from this program with your family and friends. If your debt load has become overwhelming and unmanageable, then you have turned to the right source for guidance. This book will show you how it is possible to get out from under a pile of debt while still maintaining your sanity.

Welcome to the first day of your supercharged life! I know that right now you may be feeling scared, possibly intimidated and even overwhelmed at the prospect of getting out of debt. Don't let your fears hold you back from getting out of debt, instead lean on my guidance, learn from my journey. Rest assured that if I was able to pay off my debt while being unemployed for eighteen months of my journey, then you can do it too! I strongly believe that you can get out of debt once you are armed with the tools that I lay out for you in my Supercharged Debt Repayment Plan (SDRP). All you need is the right mindset and a deep-seated desire to be free from the shackles of your debt. Also, if you are ready to take control of your financial destiny, and start creating wealth, then this book is for you too!

FALSE BELIEFS ABOUT DEBT

There are a number of false beliefs about debt, and here are a few of them:

- It is too hard to get out of debt.

- Debt is a normal way of life and there is nothing wrong with having debt, as long as you can afford your monthly payments.

- Everyone is in debt so it must not be that bad.

- The cost of living is so high that it is impossible to go through life without accumulating debt.

- Credit is required to travel and enjoy the finer things in life; therefore, one must be prepared to get into debt to enjoy the luxuries of life.

THE TRUTH ABOUT DEBT

Taking the necessary steps to get out of debt is not difficult in itself; however, changing your mindset to focus on getting out of debt can be a challenge.

Debt has not always been a normal way of life. It is only in recent history that society has encouraged and praised a consumption-oriented lifestyle that has resulted in many individuals and families living heavily in debt. Frugality and financial restraint were the norm in the first half of the twentieth century.

Debt has become more prevalent, which has resulted in more people struggling to meet their day-to-day financial needs. The sheer fact that more people are in debt does not make it acceptable. If you can't pay your bills, and you find yourself overwhelmed by your debt, then your debt is a serious problem that needs to be resolved.

The cost of living in North America is on the rise, and it is more important than ever to focus on paying off your debt by managing the way you spend your money. It is time to start living within your means without having to reach for credit to tide you over.

The finer things in life are reserved for those who have the disposable income available to pay for such luxuries, and are not available to those who are financing their consumption by accumulating credit card and other types of debt.

TYPES OF DEBT

Before we begin the SDRP program, let's look at the types of liabilities that are typically classified as debt. These debts include consumer debt, personal debt and debt owed to a government or quasi-government body (i.e. property taxes owed to a local government). While there are other types of debt owed by individuals, the following list outlines the most common types:

- Credit Card Debt

- Payday Loans

- Car Loan/Car Leasing Debt

- Revolving Lines of Credit, Home Equity Lines of Credit (HELOC)

- Student Loan Debt

- Instalment Loan Debt

- Personal Loan Debt Owed to Family and/or Friends

- Mortgage Debt

- Outstanding Taxes Owed to the Government

- Overdraft Funds Owed to a bank

- Any Outstanding Bill (i.e. Utilities, Cell Phone, Cable) that is in arrears.

In this book I lay out the steps you need to take to get out of the various types of debt, as outlined above. I have followed each one of the steps and can attest that the program works. I applied these steps in my own life and was able to pay off a large amount of debt in a relatively short period of time. Also, once I had paid off all my debt, I was able to use the same successful SDRP strategy to accumulate wealth. I call the wealth creation arm of my plan the Supercharged Wealth Accumulation Plan (SWAP).

I know that if you are reading this book you are probably struggling with debt, and are finding it difficult to repay your debt. Otherwise, you would not have purchased this book. You will have to think outside the box, and think big by believing that you will pay off all your debt. Though it may be hard to believe now, not only will you be able to pay off your debt, you will also accumulate wealth and secure your financial future.

I am proof that the SDRP and SWAP strategies work and I'm thrilled that I'm debt free (including mortgage debt free), and financially secure today because I made the important decision to get out of debt. I followed the steps of my **SDRP** strategy, and then made the equally important decision to apply the **SWAP** strategy once all my liabilities were paid off.

There is no better time than now to get out of debt. The best person to manage your money will always be you, and the way you are going to get out of debt is by managing your money wisely. I will help you transform your life by showing you the steps to get out of debt, and by showing you how to build your wealth through the SWAP strategy. You must make a commitment to yourself to take control of your financial destiny and resolve to live a debt free life starting right now.

There is no one out there who cares more about your financial well-being, and your financial future more than you.

As long as you follow the instructions in each step, you increase your chances of getting out of debt and accumulating wealth that will secure your financial future. However, if you choose to skip a step or ignore the details outlined in the steps, then you may not be able to achieve your debt-repayment goals through this plan. Since you have made the wise decision to purchase this book, I believe that you are ready to begin the **Supercharged Debt Repayment Plan (SDRP)** and the **Supercharged Wealth Accumulation Plan (SWAP)**. You have begun your journey, and I am rooting for you to succeed. Let's begin!

CHAPTER 1

STEP 1: Debt Motivation Statement

*It takes as much energy to
wish as it does to plan.*
—ELEANOR ROOSEVELT

Most people think that debt elimination is strictly a
mathematical game, but it's not! There's a huge emotional and psychological component to getting out of
debt. In fact, you need to prepare yourself to be in the
right mindset to embark on your debt repayment journey. I personally had to shift my thinking and get into
the right mindset in order to change my pre-established
money habits and financial beliefs. Creating your Debt
Motivation Statement is the most important step you
will take on your debt elimination journey, and it boils
down to asking yourself one simple question: "Why have
I decided to get out of debt?" These nine simple words will

help you determine what is motivating you to get out of debt. If you are unable to answer why you're embarking on this journey, I recommend that you stop reading right now and find one thing that will motivate you to get out of debt.

You need to find the one thing in your life that will get you into the right mindset to crush your debt. For example, are you motivated to get out of debt because if you fail to do so you could potentially lose your home, either through eviction or foreclosure? Maybe you're motivated to get out of debt because you're ready to pursue your dream of starting your own business, but need the financial security that a debt free life will afford you in order to make your dream a reality? Maybe you're close to retiring, and need to pay off your liabilities in order to have a comfortable retirement. Is it your dream to pay for your kid's education, but your excessive financial obligations mean that you don't have enough money at the end of the month to contribute towards their education? Maybe it's been your lifelong dream to take a sabbatical from work, and spend an entire year exploring and travelling the world—and you can't be saddled with debt to realize this dream. Have you just graduated from college, and desperately want to take your dream vacation? If so, the only way you can responsibly do this is to first pay off your liabilities. Finally, maybe you're currently a two income family, and are motivated to eliminate debt so that you have the option to have one spouse stay at home full-time, and care for the kids.

My Debt Motivation Statement was "to attain financial freedom, so I would never have to rely on a creditor or employer for my financial future." I was ready to take my financial destiny into my own hands. Whatever it is that motivates you, I want you to focus on that one thing that really drives you and makes you excited to take the necessary steps to annihilate your debt. Once you have determined your biggest motivator to get out of debt, you must then make a commitment to become mentally, physically and spiritually ready to pay off your debt.

To stay on course during your debt repayment journey, you will need to write down your Debt Motivation Statement on a piece of paper (please use paper for this exercise; do not input your Debt Motivation Statement on a tablet, smartphone, computer or other electronic device), and post the paper in a high-traffic location in your home. Every time you walk past your Debt Motivation Statement I want you to stop what you are doing, and take the time to read it out loud, not once but at least three times. Why read it three times? Because the more you read it, the more it will stick! This simple but crucial step will help keep you focused throughout your debt repayment journey. Once you have completed this step, you are ready to begin your journey to a debt free life.

Your Debt Motivation Statement in Step 1 is the most important step in your debt repayment journey. It is time now to stand in your truth and face your debt demons head on.

Once you have established your Debt Motivation Statement, you'll be able to face your debt demons head on. The debt demons are unforgiving, and show up in many ways. The debt demons show up in your life both on a physical and spiritual level.

The inability to sleep soundly at night is one way that debt negatively impacts your physical well-being. If you find yourself tossing and turning throughout the night, and you're constantly thinking about your debt during your waking hours, this is one way that debt is manifesting on a physical level, and you can only continue on this path for so long.

Also, if you feel out of alignment and disconnected from your true self, then you are experiencing the impact that debt is having on your spiritual well-being. Prior to beginning my Supercharged Financial Strategy, I felt like I was detached from my true self. I was unable to live in the present moment, and unable to connect with my life's purpose, because my liabilities were all I could think about. Constantly thinking about my financial obligations was causing me great stress, and I was unable to tap into my natural state of inner peace and happiness. In fact, my outlook for my future was so clouded at the beginning of my journey that I could not even comprehend what steps I needed to take to crush the debt. As a result, the interest on my debt was growing rapidly due to my inability to take the required action to pay it off. I was constantly looking externally for the solution to my debt problem, and found out soon enough that I needed to go within to find the solution.

Since I was unemployed for the first eighteen months of my debt repayment journey, I had way too much time on my hands, which meant that I had way too much time to stress out about my debt. Having over $70,000 of consumer debt to pay off while being laid off was scary, to say the least. While I was really grateful that my husband was working at the time, I was fearful of our ability to manage our financial obligations on his income alone. We had already been struggling to meet our financial obligations on two incomes, now we were forced to meet those obligations on his $30,000 a year salary. I didn't know how we were going to do it. In fact, I remember on many occasions staying up late at night, and sometimes until the early hours of the morning, just poring over my credit card statements and other debt obligations. I was scared at the prospects of losing our home, and potentially having to claim bankruptcy. During those days, I didn't have an emergency fund, I was overdrawn on my chequing account, I had a negative net worth, and I had no clue where the money was going to come from to pay off all the debt. My main objective during those long sleepless nights was to try and figure out how I was going to pay it all off. Once I began to look inward for the answer to my debt dilemma, I figured out a solution by creating the SDRP and SWAP strategies. (Both of these strategies fall under what I call the Supercharged Financial Strategy). I'm convinced that creating the Supercharged Financial Strategy has played a huge role in helping me regain my overall quality of life, and has contributed to the financial peace that I now have as a result of being debt free and financially secure. It's absolutely possible for you to attain this level of financial peace and security too, and I am here to show you how!

I am now pursuing my passion and living my life's purpose, and have the SDRP and SWAP strategies to thank for that. Implementing the SDRP and SWAP strategies allowed me to get rid of over $70,000 of consumer debt, it allowed me to pay off over $320,000 on my home, and it allowed me to build a seven figure net worth. I am super excited to show you how to implement these strategies, so that you can crush your debt and build life-changing wealth too!

CHAPTER 2

STEP 2: Get to Know Your Debt

*Whatever the mind of man can
conceive and believe, it can achieve.*
—NAPOLEON HILL

Now that you have completed your Debt Motivation Statement, and are totally motivated and on board with getting out of debt, you need to stop using all forms of credit before moving forward. You need to immediately stop using your credit cards, stop writing cheques from your line of credit, stop applying for any new loans, stop dipping into your overdraft protection from your chequing account, and stop taking any further actions that will increase the amount of debt that you owe. Essentially, you need to stop accumulating all forms of new debt, and stop using all forms of credit that are available to you. The bottom line is that in order for you to get out of debt, you need to make a commitment to have NO NEW DEBT!

Before we dive right into step 2, I want to congratulate you on completing Step 1, which I mentioned previously was the most important step in your journey. Step 2 is very important as well, but in a different way. Step 2 is where the real work begins, because it requires you to stand in your truth, and face the reality of how much you owe.

Upon completing step 2, your debt will be listed in your SDRP Schedule, a spreadsheet summarizing all of your debt. Prior to listing all your debt on a spreadsheet, you need to move ahead with the following key action plan, which will give you a complete picture of the total amount of debt that you owe:

- Contact all of the credit reporting agencies in your country and request a free credit report. I have learned from personal experience that there may be discrepancies in the data that is reported to different agencies. Sometimes lenders only report to one agency and fail to report to all agencies. That is why you need to order your reports from all the agencies located in your area. If you live in Canada or the United States, the two major credit-reporting agencies are Equifax and TransUnion, and a third agency called Experian can also be found in the United States and United Kingdom. Here is the contact information for the various credit reporting agencies in various parts of the world:

- Canada—www.equifax.ca and www.transunion.ca

- United States—www.equifax.com, www.transunion. com, and www.experian.com

- United Kingdom—www.equifax.co.uk, www. experian.co.uk and www.callcredit.co.uk

- Europe—There are a lot of credit reporting agencies in Europe and since these agencies existed prior to the formation of the European Union, they serve the respective European country in which they reside. For example, the reporting agency in the Netherlands is Stichting Bureau Krediet Registratie. You can find it at www.bkr.nl

- You are able to get free credit reports in both Canada and the US. However, in the US you can only pull one free credit report each year from the respective credit reporting agencies. (That works out to three reports each year, which means you can get one free report from each agency.)

Once you receive your credit reports, you need to review them closely to ensure there are no errors or omissions on the reports. If you discover an error or omission, you need to follow the instructions that are included in the credit report documents that you receive from the credit-reporting agency, and take the outlined steps provided to correct the error or omission.

Now that all your outstanding debts have been verified, your next step is to call each one of your lenders to confirm the following information:

- Outstanding balance;

- The annual interest rate on the debt (also called annual percentage rate or APR);

- The minimum payment and due date on the most recent statement.

SECURED AND UNSECURED DEBT

You are almost ready to begin inputting the details to your SDRP schedule, but first I want to discuss the difference between secured and unsecured debt. Secured debt is debt that is backed by collateral, or a hard asset. For example, a mortgage or car loan is considered a secured debt because the physical asset, your home or car, acts as collateral for the loan that is extended to you. Therefore, if you were to ever default on a secured debt, the bank can take back the collateral, which means that if you defaulted on your mortgage, the bank can initiate foreclosure proceedings, and sell your home to recoup any loss they may have incurred. In some jurisdictions banks have the right to sue previous homeowners for any outstanding balance that is still owed on a home after foreclosure proceedings have been completed.

On the other hand, credit card debt or any debt that is not backed by collateral—for example, student loans, unsecured line of credits, personal loans, medical bills, and payday loans—is unsecured debt, because there is no underlying asset, or collateral, that backs it up. Credit cards, and other unsecured debt, have higher interest rates than secured debt, such as mortgages, since the lender is taking on substantially more risk to extend this type of credit to a borrower.

PRIORITIZING MONTHLY DEBT PAYMENTS

There is typically a hierarchy when it comes to the priority in which you pay back your debt. Legally speaking, secured debt takes priority over unsecured debt. However, practically speaking you want to consider the necessity of the debt, and the human and legal ramifications of not paying off a debt when determining your debt obligations.

First, always make the minimum payments on your mortgage and car loans each and every month. Many bankruptcy lawyers and consumer debt professionals categorize mortgages and car loans as "necessities" since failure to make these payments will result in you losing your home or having your car repossessed.

Second, you want to make sure that you pay all debts that are your legal obligations, such as taxes owed to the government and outstanding child support payments. This is very important since these obligations cannot be discharged in bankruptcy and you want to avoid having your wages garnisheed in the event of a default on either one of these obligations. I would also include student loans on the second priority list because most student loans cannot be discharged in bankruptcy. If you default on your student loan, or if the loan is in deferment (deferment means that you have asked for your debt payments to be postponed until a later date due to financial hardship and other such reasons), the interest rate on the student loan continues to accrue and you run the risk of the student loan ballooning to an unmanageable level.

Third, make sure to stay current on all your other debt, such as consumer debt. This third category of debt includes things such as credit cards, lines of credit, and any other personal loan that you owe. It's important to note that student loans are often included in the category of consumer debt.

Most financial professionals will agree that the third category of debt should be paid off in the order of debt with the highest interest rate first, and debt with the lowest interest rate last. Prioritizing debt repayments in this order, from highest to lowest interest rates makes sense if you are only approaching this exercise strictly from a mathematical perspective. However, it actually makes more sense from a human psychology perspective to tackle the smallest debt balance first, because people are emotionally motivated when it comes to their finances. Successfully paying off the smallest debt in a short period of time will motivate you to tackle the next liability. I base my SDRP strategy on a method that is more aligned with human psychology, and will discuss this method, along with the second debt repayment method, later in this chapter.

LIST YOUR DEBTS

Now it's time to list ALL of your debt on a spreadsheet. In the list that you prepare, ensure to include columns for the outstanding balance, the annual interest rate, the minimum payment and the due date for each one of your credit cards, car loans, student loans and any other debt that you owe. If you have a mortgage, list your mortgage on the debt repayment schedule, however, you can choose to tackle that debt at the end of your debt repayment journey, since it is most likely the largest debt that you owe. I ultimately applied the SDRP strategy to my mortgage *after* I had paid off all my consumer debt (consumer debt includes debt such as credit card debt, student loans, car loans, personal loans, and lines of credit).

If you have a home equity line of credit (HELOC) that currently has a balance, then this debt must also be listed on the spreadsheet. A HELOC fits the definition of consumer debt, and accordingly, must be eliminated along with all other consumer debt that is outstanding.

DEBT REPAYMENT METHODS

There are two methods of paying off debt—**the debt snowball method and the debt avalanche method.** The debt snowball method involves listing obligations on your spreadsheet in order from the smallest balance to the largest balance, and the avalanche method entails listing liabilities from highest interest rate to lowest interest rate. The avalanche method makes more sense when viewed strictly from a mathematical perspective —you apply any extra resources to your debt with the highest interest rate first, so that you end up paying less interest over the course of the payment plan.

As mentioned previously, I learned that there is a huge psychological and emotional component to getting out of debt—I needed to see immediate results in order to stay motivated on my Supercharged Financial journey. Therefore, I decided to use the debt snowball method to get out of debt. The debt snowball method was effective for me and it helped me get out of over $70,000 of consumer debt in just under three years, and it helped me pay off my mortgage. It allowed me to experience success quickly, which improved my emotional state and lowered my stress levels. It also provided me with the quick psychological reward of paying off my first bill in just three months.

I know many financial experts out there are strong believers in the debt avalanche method (paying off your highest interest debt first), but they often fail to take into account the very important fact that people are typically driven by emotions, beliefs and behavioural triggers, rather than being driven by hard science and logical reasoning. And, I am proof that the snowball method works, and is highly effective for those of us who need to see immediate results. I will be focusing exclusively on the debt snowball method in this book.

The snowball method of repaying your debts can provide immediate results that can boost your confidence.

Eliminating my debt with the smallest balance within three short months of starting the plan gave me the boost of confidence I needed to become more committed, confident and positively charged to tackle the next debt on my list. With this new-found focus and drive, I consistently made monthly payments towards each debt, and was able to make my last consumer debt payment less than three years after implementing the SDRP strategy. Once my consumer debt was paid off, I implemented the SWAP strategy, which provided me with access to the funds required to pay off my mortgage. In fact, my mortgage was paid off thirteen years sooner than the scheduled payoff date!

My goal for this book is to help you channel the

confidence, focus and drive, and mindset shift that are required to achieve your debt free and wealth building status, in the same way that I was able to. Follow the steps that I lay out for you and begin living a fuller, more enriched life, spending your life energy on your passion and pursuits that matter the most to you. By following the Supercharged Financial Strategy, you will stop constantly worrying about your debt, and will begin feeling empowered and in complete control of your financial life. The Supercharged Financial Strategy worked for me, and it will work for you too!

A WORD ABOUT CREDIT CARDS

Once you confirm the minimum monthly payment for each one of your credit card debts, enter this figure on your debt spreadsheet, which at this point should list all the liabilities you owe. You will use this figure as the ongoing minimum payment for each outstanding debt.

It's important that you call each one of your lenders on the same date. The amount of outstanding debt on every credit card on a particular date is the information that will form the basis of your SDRP schedule. Also, if you have been making payments on time, and are not delinquent on any payments, take an extra step and negotiate a lower annual interest rate: ask your lenders to reduce the annual interest rate on your revolving debt (i.e. credit cards, lines of credit, department store cards etc.). A poll that was conducted by CreditCards. com found that three out of four people who asked for a reduction on their credit card interest rate were successful. Everybody should be asking for this benefit, but only about 23% of credit card holders currently ask for this perk, according to the CreditCards.com poll. This one step can save you hundreds of dollars in interest costs, or even more depending on the amount of debt you carry.

Once you begin paying down your debt, and not incurring new debts, (remember that you have stopped using your credit cards once you begin the SDRP program), you will notice that the monthly minimum payment required by the credit card (and line of credit companies) begins to steadily decline. Credit card companies and other lenders of revolving debt DO NOT want you to make the same minimum payment every month. Instead, they want you to use their minimum payment guideline because it serves their bottom line and keeps you on the debt treadmill for much longer.

DO NOT pay attention to the credit card companies lower minimum payment requirements; instead, keep paying the minimum payment that you establish at the beginning of the SDRP program. By freezing your minimum payment you will be paying off all your debts at a faster rate and will be debt free sooner.

> **Credit card companies and other lenders of revolving debt DO NOT want you to make the same minimum payment every month.**

You can take the additional step of asking your lender if they have any promotional interest rate offers available on their credit card or line of credit. The best balance transfer credit card offers that are on the market in Canada and the US at the time of writing this book are 0% annual interest rate offers for terms that range from three months to as long as eighteen months. If you are considering transferring a balance from one lender to another to take advantage of any promotional offers, make sure that before signing up you are aware of the balance transfer fees associated with each offer. (Balance transfer fees range from as low as 1% to as high as 5% of the total balance transferred.) Also, only transfer the amount of debt that you can comfortably pay off within the promotional low-interest rate period. Credit card companies are not offering you these rates because they are your friends or because they care about you. Not a chance! They are hoping that you will make a mistake by not paying your monthly bill on time or that you will not be able to pay off your entire balance prior to the expiry of the low interest rate promotional period. Should you make this error, the credit card company can charge their regular interest rates on any unpaid balance.

Please note that if you are currently in default on your credit cards or any other debt, or if you have an outstanding payment due on any obligation, and that outstanding obligation has been reported to a credit reporting agency, you will NOT be able to successfully negotiate lower interest rates or promotional balance transfer offers with your lenders. However, you may be able to make a debt settlement with your lenders and negotiate a reduced payment schedule on your debt. Please refer to the sections "Consumer Proposals" and "Debt Settlements" in Chapter 8 for further guidance on the debt settlement process.

At this point you should have in front of you a list of all the outstanding debts that you owe, the name of your lenders, the respective interest rate, the monthly minimum payment associated with each debt, and the payment due date. Your list of debts would look similar to the sample list provided below.

TABLE 1. **SAMPLE LIST OF OUTSTANDING DEBTS**

Lender	Balance Owing	Interest Rate	Minimum Monthly Payment	Payment Due Date
Visa	$1,000	8.99%	$20	Jan 5
Student Loan	$3,800	5.5%	$81	Jan 15
MasterCard	$5,000	19.9%	$100	Jan 25
Personal Loan From Parents	$8,000	0%	$130	Jan 30
Auto Loan	$10,000	8.5%	$355.35	Jan 30
TOTAL:	$27,800	N/A	$686.35	

Two Important Points

- **Make sure that you always pay your credit card balance transfers on time!** I cannot emphasize this enough, as some balance transfer offers will automatically be cancelled if a payment is made late, and you will have incurred additional interest charges due to the promotional rate being replaced with an onerous regular credit card rate that can be as high as 26% in some cases.

- **Any outstanding debts that are owed to family and friends should be on your outstanding debt list.** It is the honourable thing to do. The worst thing you can do is to take a loan from someone who is close to you and not pay it back. This will cause a terrible rift in the relationship, which often cannot be repaired.

Great job on completing the above action items! You are now ready to move to the next step.

CHAPTER 3

STEP 3: SDRP Debt Repayment Schedule

> My experience has taught me that
> a normal person can accomplish anything
> possible of human accomplishment,
> through the aid of the human mind.
>
> —NAPOLEON HILL

Now that all your outstanding debt is listed on a spreadsheet, it's time to enter the information into the **SDRP Debt Repayment Schedule**. I will show you how to create the **SDRP** Debt Repayment Schedule, but you can begin by organizing the list of debts from the smallest balance to the largest. You can also make some small modifications to the spreadsheet you have created in Step 2 wherein you listed all your debt, so that it becomes your **SDRP** Debt Repayment Schedule. Please make sure that your **SDRP** Debt Repayment Schedule lists all your secured and unsecured debt. Therefore, if you have a mortgage, include the mortgage debt on your SDRP Schedule, with the understanding that your mortgage will most likely be the last debt that you pay off.

This system is based on paying the minimum monthly payment on each debt listed on the SDRP Debt Repayment Schedule, with the exception of the bill with the smallest balance. In addition to paying the minimum payment on the bill with the smallest balance, you will apply extra money towards this debt. The extra money that you will apply to this debt will come from the money that you have once you implement all the tips and strategies that I provide to reduce your monthly expenses. I also want you to apply any type of windfall that you receive—a bonus from work, a tax refund, Christmas money, birthday money, a pay raise or promotion, a rebate from the purchase of an item, money acquired from selling your belongings—you get the idea. This is effectively the way you begin to supercharge your debt repayments.

This is the way that I was able to supercharge my debt repayment and pay off over $70,000 of debt in less than three years, and pay off over $320,000 on my home in 12 years. DO NOT make the same mistakes as many people when they come across a windfall—blow the windfall on a discretionary consumer product, spend it on a vacation that they cannot afford, or unknowingly split the windfall evenly amongst all outstanding debts.

The most effective method I used when encountering a windfall during my debt repayment days was to apply my entire windfall to the debt with the smallest balance. By concentrating your debt efforts on the smallest debt first (and strategically paying off the debt with the largest balance last), you will be motivated to stay the course and you will be successful in reaching your goals. By the way, if your windfall is particularly large (i.e. a sizable bonus from work), you may find yourself in the very fortunate position of paying off all your liabilities well in advance of your scheduled debt payoff date. Now that should be enough motivation to apply your windfall money towards paying off your debt!

Once the debt with the smallest balance is paid off, you will then take the minimum payment from that liability and add it to the minimum payment of the next debt on the list. This action will supercharge the speed at which you pay back your liabilities because you are now combining the minimum payment of the liability that has just been paid off with the minimum payment of the next debt on the list, which results in you paying back your debt faster.

In addition to systematically rolling over the minimum payment from the last paid off debt, you are also applying all your windfall money towards the debt with the lowest outstanding balance. This is why I call this the *Supercharged* Debt Repayment Plan. Methodically following this process will guarantee your success.

This system forces you to pay larger amounts towards your debts, and gets you to debt free status sooner than you could have ever imagined. By religiously repeating this step over and over again, you will pay off every last one of your debts! By the way, the very last debt listed on your debt repayment schedule will be paid off so fast that you will most likely have extra money left over after the last payment. The reason that you'll most likely have extra money left over, is due to the rollover feature of the snowball method. Namely, your last debt payment will be paid off with money that is the total of all the previous minimum payments. That means you will have a lot of money to contribute towards your last debt payment. The difference between your last debt payment and the money you have available to contribute towards that last debt payment will be the extra funds left over. The extra money that I had left over after making my last debt payment was applied towards a trip that my husband and I took as a reward for paying off over $70,000 of debt. We ended up paying cash for a trip to Hawaii! I highly recommend that once you pay off your consumer debt, you take some of your extra money and reward yourself in whatever way that you see fit—just make sure to use cash to fund that reward! However, I want you to apply the rest of that money towards your emergency fund (I will discuss how to build up your emergency fund in Step 6.)

Here is a sample of how your SDRP Debt Repayment Schedule would look:

TABLE 2. **SDRP DEBT REPAYMENT SCHEDULE**

Lender	Total Balance Owed	Interest Rate	Minimum Monthly Payment	Super-charged Extra Payment	Total Payment
1. Visa	$1,000	8.99%	$20	$200	$220
2. Student Loan	$3,800	5.5%	$81		$81
3. MasterCard	$5,000	19.9%	$100		$100
4. Personal Loan From Parents	$8,000	0%	$130		$130
5. Auto Loan	$10,000	8.5%	$355.35		$355.35
TOTAL:	$27,800	TOTAL: $686.35		TOTAL Inc. Extra Pmt.: $886.35	

After five months of following the SDRP strategy, this is how your SDRP Debt Repayment Schedule would look:

TABLE 3. **SDRP DEBT REPAYMENT SCHEDULE AT FIVE MONTHS**

Lender	Total Balance Owed	Interest Rate	Minimum Monthly Payment	Super-charged Extra Payment	Total Payment
1. Visa	$0	8.99%	$0	$0	PAID OFF
2. Student Loan	$3,800	5.5%	$101	200	$301
3. MasterCard	$5,000	19.9%	$100		$100
4. Personal Loan From Parents	$8,000	0%	$130		$130
5. Auto Loan	$10,000	8.5%	$355.35		$355.35
TOTAL:	$26,800	TOTAL: $686.35		TOTAL Inc. Extra Pmt.: $886.35	

If you're not interested in creating your own SDRP schedule, then I recommend you use a debt repayment calculator offered by a company named Vertex42.com (the company name is also the website address). For a nominal fee, this company offers a great debt repayment calculator that helps you prepare an in-depth debt repayment schedule, which incorporates all elements of the SDRP strategy. Make sure that when you visit the site you click on the "debt payoff" option, then click on the image that reads "debt reduction calculator," and purchase the "personal use only" version of the debt repayment calculator, which costs $9.95 as of the date of writing this section of the book.

Below is an example of how the Vertex42.com debt repayment calculator would look based on the debts listed in the sample SDRP schedule outlined in Table 3 of this chapter.

TABLE 4. SAMPLE SDRP USING THE VERTEX42.COM DEBT REPAYMENT CALCULATOR

Supercharged Debt Repayment Plan

Name: Jane Doe

Prepared by: Money Corp.
[Company Name]

Balance Date: 1/1/2015

[Address, City ST ZIP]
Phone: [Phone]

Creditor Information Table

Row	Creditor	Balance	Rate	Payment	Custom	Interest-only
1	Visa	1,000.00	8.99%	20.00	2	7.50
2	Student Loan	3,800.00	5.50%	81.00	1	17.42
3	MasterCard	5,000.00	19.90%	100.00	3	82.92
4	Personal Loan (Parents	8,000.00	0.00%	130.00	5	0.00
5	Auto Loan	10,000.00	8.50%	355.35	4	70.84
6						0.00
7						0.00
8						0.00
9						0.00
10						0.00
	Total:	27,800.00		Total:	686.35	

Monthly Payment 686.35 *Too Low*
Initial Snowball $ 200.00   **Strategy:** Snowball (Lowest Balance First) ▼

Results are only estimates

Creditors in Chosen Order	Original Balance	Total Interest Paid	Months to Pay Off	Month Paid Off
Visa	1,000.00	192.36	33	Oct-17
Student Loan	3,800.00	429.18	37	Feb-18
MasterCard	5,000.00	3,113.55	45	Oct-18
Personal Loan (Parents	8,000.00	-	48	Jan-19
Auto Loan	10,000.00	1,192.47	32	Sep-17
	-	-	-	
	-	-	-	
	-	-	-	
	-	-	-	
Total Interest Paid:		**4,927.56** (Lower is Better)		

Source: Vertex42.com

For details on how to use the Vertex42.com debt repayment calculator to prepare your SDRP schedule, go to YouTube and search "Vertex 42 Debt Reduction Calculator," and watch the tutorial video.

CHAPTER 4

STEP 4: Develop a Money Management System

The only way you will ever permanently take control of your financial life is to dig deep and fix the root problem.

—SUZE ORMAN

At this point you may be asking yourself—how am I going to find the money to pay off my debt? Step 4 provides you with an action plan that lays out how you will find the money to pay off your debt. It boils down to figuring out how much you are willing to sacrifice to get out of debt.

Setting up a budget is the most sensible way to successfully pay off all your debt. It is also a crucial step in the SDRP strategy that will allow you to organize your finances in a way that will help you find the money to pay off your debt. Also, once you create your budget you will begin applying a pre-determined amount of money towards your *emergency fund* each month. Setting up an emergency fund is one of the most critical parts of the SDRP and SWAP strategies because it ensures that you will never have to turn to a credit card or revolving line of credit to take care of any unexpected financial emergencies. (Step 6 of the Supercharged Financial Strategy outlines the creation of your emergency fund in more detail.)

Here are the steps to follow when you create your budget and find the extra money to apply to your SDRP program:

1. Set your goals and priorities.

2. Track your spending and cut your expenses.

3. Create your budget.

4. Maximize your debt repayment program.

SET YOUR GOALS AND PRIORITIES

Setting financial goals helps you stay on the right path throughout your debt free journey and forces you to stay focused on your desired outcome. Determine your primary objective for getting out of debt and put your goals in writing. Here are some questions you can ask yourself to determine your goals:

- "Am I getting out of debt so I can finally start saving money to buy a house?"

- "Do I need to pay off my debt so I can start my own business?"

- "Am I getting out of debt so I can begin saving for retirement?"

- "Do I need to get out of debt so I can help my children pay for their education?"

Like I did, you may find that you simply want to get out of debt because you are just sick and tired of being in debt. You have reached your breaking point; you are ready to tackle your debt and take control of your financial destiny. Once I reached my financial breaking point, I was able to shift my mindset and get serious about accomplishing my debt free goals.

I had lost my job and I was sick and tired of being in debt up to my eyeballs. I knew there was a better way to live. My breaking point came when I called the customer service department of my Visa card and asked the representative for a credit limit increase. During that time in my life, I was maxed out on my Visa and had virtually no money in my bank account. I did not have an emergency fund at the time, and planned on using the extra "money" from the Visa credit limit increase to tide us over until I found a new job. I literally had no cash reserves to bail us out in the event of a financial emergency. In fact, I had dipped into the overdraft protection on my chequing account and had a negative balance in that account. The Visa card company rejected my request for a credit limit increase. The rejection from the Visa company changed my life for the better, and was a turning point in my financial life.

It dawned on me at that moment that I could no longer rely on my credit cards as an emergency fund. In fact, I got mad at myself for relying so heavily on credit cards and other forms of credit to rescue me during financial emergencies. Cash is the ONLY source for building an emergency fund. This Visa experience contributed to me shifting my financial mindset from that of scarcity to abundance. I made a commitment to myself to take full control of my financial destiny, and vowed to do everything in my power to become financially independent.

I vowed that I would get out of debt and would never be at the mercy of a lender again. I would never allow a lender to have so much control over my life. I was done being a prisoner to my lenders. The reference to being a prisoner to my lenders may sound a bit extreme but I truly was at the mercy of all my lenders during this time in my life. And, if you are currently in debt, you are now a prisoner of your lenders. It's time to break the chains and set yourself free.

Your debt free journey will be much more successful when you understand what is motivating you to get out of debt.

Whatever your reason for getting out of debt, make sure that you write down your goals. Written goals have a greater chance of becoming reality versus goals that you note mentally. You need to keep your goals at the forefront of your mind. Keeping your goals front and centre will help you get through the tough times when you feel weary or frustrated and want to give up. If you fail to set your goals and objectives now, you may risk your chance of successfully paying off your debt, and may fall back into old budget-busting financial habits.

If there are various reasons why you are getting out of debt, prioritize them from most important to least important. This will also help you stay focused on the most important reasons you are embarking on this journey.

Once you have established your goals, you need to take the time to write them down. In fact, I want you to write down your goals and Debt Motivation Statement (which you completed in Step 1) in a *money journal*. A money journal is like a typical journal; however, instead of writing about your day-to-day life events, you write about your day-to-day financial events. For example, in the next section of this book, I want you to keep track of your daily spending habits, and I want you to use the money journal to do this. I will discuss the money journal concept in a bit more detail in the next section.

In Chapter 1, I recommended that you write down your Debt Motivation Statement on a Post-it note, and then proceed to stick it in a high-traffic location in your home. I'm going to recommend that you do the same exercise but this time, you are completing this exercise for all your goals. Namely, I want you to write your goals on a piece of paper, preferably a large Post-it note, and post the paper on a wall located in a high-traffic area of your home. Make sure to organize your goals in the order of importance, with the most important goal being listed as number one, and the least important goal being listed last. This will literally work to etch your goals into your subconscious mind and will help contribute to the successful completion of your Supercharged Financial Strategy.

MAKE A VISION BOARD

As I noted earlier in this book, there is a huge psychological component to getting out of debt, and if you are open to shifting your money mindset and money beliefs, you will increase your likelihood of success. One tool you can use to shift your money mindset and beliefs, and increase your chances of successfully completing the SDRP program, is a vision board. A vision board provides a visual image of your goals. Find photos of your goals in magazines or on websites. (Pinterest is a great social media platform for vision board photos.) Post these images of words, photos or symbols on your vision board.

On my own vision board I posted motivational phrases and quotes along with photos. These phrases and photos kept me motivated and helped to lift my spirits when I was tempted to veer off my plan. I actually took it one step further and often mentally repeated some of the goals that I wanted to accomplish in my daily meditation.

Remember to post goals on your vision board that can be achieved once you get out of debt, and constantly reference your vision board to remind yourself of why you have decided to take this journey. For example, if your goal is to buy a home in a few years, and you need to get rid of your debt to save for a down payment, this is the message that you would post on your vision board: "I will buy my house in 3 years, and put a 20 percent down payment on my home." You need to preface the statement as if what you want to happen has already occurred. That is the point of a vision board—it helps you express your dreams and goals in a way that you will begin to manifest what you desire into your life. Also, make sure to mentally visualize your goals at every opportunity you get. Vision boards and visualization techniques will help you stay on track to successfully pay off your debt and achieve your goals. Take it from me, these tools work!

Visualization is a technique whereby you mentally focus on positive images that are directly related to the goals you wish to achieve.

TRACK YOUR SPENDING AND CUT YOUR EXPENSES

To find the money you need for your SDRP, you need to review your spending, and find ways to cut your monthly expenses. Cutting your monthly expenditures can free up cash to put towards your SDRP, which means that you will be debt free sooner than you imagined. Successfully completing your SDRP requires you to be aware of how you are spending your money day to day. Proceed with the following steps as it relates to your monthly income and expenses:

- Monthly Income: Calculate all the sources of income you receive monthly, which may include net take-home pay, child support payments, rental income, or investment income (i.e. dividend payments), to name a few examples.

- Monthly Fixed Expenses: Calculate all your monthly fixed expenses which may include rent or mortgage payment, auto loan payment, property taxes, home and auto insurance premiums, as examples.

• Monthly Variable Expenses: Calculate all your monthly variable expenses such as groceries, clothing, utilities, cell phone, and restaurant meals, to name a few.

Now input these items into a spreadsheet (similar to the spreadsheet shown in the Sample Monthly Budget below).

Your Fixed Expenses are amounts that don't typically change from month to month. Variable Expenses do change from month to month because of choices you make daily. You need to track variable expenses and see where you can find some extra cash.

To get an accurate picture of your variable expenses, keep track of all your variable expenses in your money journal for one full month. (Begin tracking your expenses at the beginning of the month, as opposed to starting a thirty-day tracking period mid-month, so that you get a more accurate picture of how much you spend in any given month.) With the money journal you can track your expenses in a physical journal, or alternatively, can use a mobile app to track your variable expenses.

Here is what you should write down in your money journal:

• The date of the purchase;

• A description of the item purchased;

• The price of the item.

You'll be surprised at how much money you're spending on frivolous items that really don't make you happy, and you'll begin to become a more conscious consumer and spender. My motto is "spend passion, cut junk." This means that you should spend your money on things that you're passionate about and things that bring you joy, and cut spending on things that don't bring you joy. It really boils down to being more mindful about your money.

A conscious spender or conscious consumer is someone who examines their spending habits and begins cutting out wasteful spending, and redirects their spending on things they value and that bring them joy.

Once you have tracked your expenses for an entire month, you will have enough information to input your variable expenses onto your monthly budget spreadsheet. If you want an even more accurate picture of your spending I would encourage you to continue tracking your variable expenses for an additional month or two. Tracking your variable expenses will allow you to really home in on your spending habits. Whether you choose to track your results over one, two or three months, carry your money journal with you for at least one full month. This is the only way that you will be able to understand where your money goes and how you can trim your spending to pay off your debt. Remember, the primary purpose of the money journal is to track your variable expenses.

You can put your own personal touch on your money journal, and get creative in the method you choose to use for your money journal. It can be as simple as a Dollar Store note pad where you jot down your daily variable expenses, as creative as a customized journal, or as tech savvy as a personal spending tracker app that you download on your smartphone. Whatever method you choose, just make sure that you are tracking your daily spending so that you can get an accurate picture of your daily spending habits over a specified period of time. The money journal will arm you with the information you need to trim your variable expenses and get out of debt fast!

Here are five tips you can implement to reduce some of your monthly expenses:

1. It's imperative that I mention again the importance of calling each one of your lenders and requesting a lower interest rate on your debt. Ask to speak with a manager or supervisor. Do not waste any time speaking with a customer service representative, as they do not have the authority to negotiate the reduction of interest rates or payment arrangements on your debt.

2. Call your home and auto insurance provider(s) to see if you can reduce your monthly premiums. The most common ways to reduce your premiums is to request an increase in your deductibles (i.e. if you currently have a $500 deductible, increase it to $1000). Also, moving all your insur-

ance policies to one provider makes you eligible for a bundling discount from the provider. You can also reduce your insurance premiums if your car is being driven for short distances (usually under 5000 miles per year if you live in the United States, and under 5000 kilometres per year if you live in Canada or other parts of the world, such as the United Kingdom). Make sure you inquire about any other discounts that may be offered such as discounts for claim free status, professional associations, group discounts, employer discounts, and discounts for tracking your driving by adding a black box to your vehicle that records your driving patterns, (this is not available in every country).

If you are successful in reducing your premium with your current insurance provider, that is wonderful; however, if your insurance provider is unable to reduce your premium, then it's time to start shopping around for new auto and home insurance, with the aim of reducing your monthly insurance premiums. Make sure that you have secured new insurance policies prior to cancelling any old policies.

3. Call your cell phone provider, and, if applicable, home phone provider and request a more cost-effective plan. You may also want to look into the possibility of ditching your landline altogether and replacing it with your cell phone. However, make sure that you do all your research to determine if cancelling your landline is the best option

for you. There may be security reasons why you still want to hold onto your landline. (Some 911 operators cannot pinpoint your location in the event of an emergency when you call from a cell phone versus a landline.)

4. Call your cable company and internet provider to see if you can switch to a lower cost plan; alternatively, if you are ready to cut the cable then proceed to cancel your cable plan and switch to an online streaming service such as Netflix or Hulu.

5. If you have a mortgage and a solid credit score (anything above 720), you may want to consider refinancing your mortgage to free up some money. Make an appointment with your mortgage company and discuss the options available. This move can save you hundreds of dollars, possibly thousands of dollars a year in mortgage interest. Make sure to factor in all the extra costs associated with refinancing prior to taking this step. While refinancing your mortgage at a lower annualized rate will bring down the costs of your mortgage payments, you need to stay in your home long enough to recoup the costs associated with refinancing. Also, be sure that you choose an amortization schedule that is shorter than, or exactly the same as the number of years remaining on your current mortgage. For example, if you currently have fifteen years remaining on your mortgage, make sure that you set up your mortgage as a fifteen-year mortgage, at the very minimum. Renegotiating a longer amortization

period will not benefit you in the long run, as this step will ultimately result in you shelling out *more* money in interest costs over the life of your mortgage.

And finally, if you are currently renting, I recommend that you start researching the rental market in your area to determine if the amount you are paying in rent is in line with the current rental rates. If you discover that the rental rates in your community are on the decline, then this is the time to begin looking at whether it makes sense to move to a less expensive home. This decision will only make sense if the savings you are afforded by moving outweigh the moving costs you will incur.

The extra money that you save by taking these actions to reduce your expenses MUST be applied towards your SDRP payments. The objective of the SDRP program is to find ways to accumulate extra money that can be applied to your debt. And it is only when you begin applying this extra money towards your liabilities that you begin to see concrete results, which will lead to you successfully becoming debt free. The benefits of the SDRP strategy will be realized by you taking these five steps to reduce your expenses.

NET MONTHLY INCOME

Now it's time to subtract your expenses from your monthly income to calculate your net monthly income. Your net monthly income will be the source of funds for your SDRP payments, and will also serve as a means of funding your emergency fund. (The emergency fund is discussed in Step 6 of the SDRP program.)

Here is a sample budget of someone who has just begun their SDRP journey, and who has not yet taken any steps to reduce their monthly expenses:

TABLE 5. **SAMPLE MONTHLY BUDGET**

INCOME

Wages (take-home) – partner 1	$5,333.32
Wages (take-home) – partner 2	
Investment dividends:	
Other:	
Total Income	**$5,333.32**

FIXED EXPENSES

These are expenses that do not change from one month to the next.

Mortgage payment	$2,709.37
Property Taxes	$245.00
Home Insurance	$30.33
Alarm System	$46.39
Utilities	$250.00
Telephone & Internet	$45.10
Cable TV	$54.59
Cell Phone	$65.00
Parking	$60.00
Transportation / Bus Pass	$92.00
Car Payment (Lease)	$715.65
Car Insurance	$79.60
Orthodontics	$168.75
Costco Membership	$8.75
Pet Insurance	$39.89
Other	
Total Fixed Expenses	**$4610.42**

VARIABLE EXPENSES

These expenses are discretionary and more easily altered.

They vary from month to month. Some can be considered little luxuries.

Personal care	
Clothing	
Entertainment and recreation	$50.00
Gifts	
Groceries	$200.00
Credit Card Payments	$1530.00
Pet Food and Treats	$130.00
Gas	$120.00
Car Maintenance	$250.00
Veterinarian Visit	$13.33
Groomers	$22.50
Doggie Bags	$2.00
Dining out	
Household expenses	
Vacations (monthly savings amount)	
Savings contributions	
Other	
Total Variable Expenses	**$2317.83**

BUDGET TOTALS

Total Income	**$5,333.32**
Total Fixed Expenses	($4610.42)
Total Variable Expenses	($2317.83)
NET INCOME	**($1,594.93)**
(Income minus Expenses)	

Sample Monthly Budget

As you can see, this sample monthly budget is not a balanced budget, nor is it a budget that can be sustained for much longer. In fact, this person is living dangerously beyond their means, and it is only a matter of time before they hit a financial brick wall. A job loss, prolonged illness, or serious financial setback will most likely result in the person either filing for bankruptcy, or sadly going deeper and deeper into debt.

This budget is in urgent need of repair and will require a focused and disciplined approach to get the monthly expenses in line with the monthly income. The fact that you are reading this book and have invested your time and money into implementing the SDRP strategy, means that you may be able to relate to the financial circumstances outlined in the sample monthly budget —there is more money going out for expenses than there is money coming in.

While your situation may not be as dire as this, relief is available to you and anyone in debt. All you have to do is begin viewing your finances as an extension of your overall health and well-being.

The close alignment between your financial health and your physical and mental health is nothing short of amazing. How many times have you lost sleep thinking about the debt that you owe? Or, maybe there was a time when you decided to use credit to buy a major consumer item (i.e. big screen TV or the latest tech gadget), and later felt sick to your stomach with buyer's remorse? Or, you may have booked a tropical vacation on a credit card knowing that you did not have the financial means to pay off the bill once the credit card statement arrived in the mail. Once the credit card statement arrives in the mail, you avoid opening it at all costs. Feelings of guilt and shame may arise when you accept the gravity of your financial situation.

In contrast, if you have worked diligently to save a healthy emergency fund and have successfully paid off your debt, you will be able to sleep soundly at night, and will have the financial means to purchase big-ticket items, take fabulous vacations, and enjoy your life on your terms. As an added bonus, you'll be able to pay for all these luxury items with cash!

In the next section I'll show you how to create a balanced budget that will help chart the path to paying off your debt, and show you how to build an emergency fund that will help take care of the unplanned events in life. You'll have the peace of mind that comes from being able to take care of your financial, physical, and mental well-being. Once you implement the steps to reduce your monthly expenses, you'll have access to more money, and will be able to apply that extra money directly to your SDRP payments.

You'll need to make some lifestyle changes in order to get to a balanced budget. You will also need to be disciplined and focused when it comes to balancing your budget. By slashing your expenses, through the elimination of unnecessary expenditures, and by creating a budget based on your needs, as opposed to your wants, you will be able to achieve your goal of paying off all your debt.

CREATE YOUR MONTHLY BUDGET

When creating your budget you need to get serious about trimming the fat from your bottom line. The secret to a successful budget is organization. I was able to create a successful monthly budget system that really helped me stay on track when it came to sticking to my SDRP strategy. Once you are able to successfully manage the due dates of your expenses, the amount owing on each expense, and the total amount due each month, you'll be well on your way to crushing your liabilities. Before you know it, you'll be converting the SDRP strategy into the SWAP strategy.

Monthly Bill Payment Schedule

When I was implementing the SDRP strategy to eliminate my debt, I decided to create a **Monthly Bill Payment Schedule** to keep track of the bills that needed to be paid each month. The Monthly Bill Payment Schedule lists for each bill the due date, a brief description of the bill, and the amount owing on each bill. Most importantly, I tracked each one of my bills, not just my credit card bills. For example, I included line items for my utility bill, my phone bill and even my insurance premium payments were added to the schedule. The point is I increased my chances of succeeding with the SDRP strategy by having a system in place that provided me with a clear picture of all my monthly payment obligations.

Here is a sample Monthly Bill Payment Schedule. I would encourage you to create your own Monthly Bill Payment schedule and begin incorporating it into your own SDRP program.

TABLE 6. **MONTHLY BILL PAYMENT SCHEDULE**

March 1, 2014	Property Taxes	$277.00
March 1, 2014	Car Insurance	$28.12
March 1, 2014	Car Insurance	$52.58
March 1, 2014	Home Insurance	$67.41
March 3, 2014	Visa	$32.02
March 3, 2014	MBNA Credit Card	$502.30
March 3, 2014	Cell Phone Bill #1	$65.34
March 6, 2014	MasterCard	$1042.23
March 7, 2014	Phone and Cable	$131.81
March 7, 2014	Mortgage	$772.31
March 11, 2014	Cell Phone Bill #2	$36.75
March 21, 2014	Line of Credit	$540.12
March 21, 2014	Mortgage	$772.31
March 31, 2014	Utilities/Water	$326.28
March 31, 2014	Natural Gas	$203.50
	TOTAL	**$4,850.08**

As soon as I began using the Monthly Bill Payment Schedule I noticed that I was paying every bill on time each month. This rather simple, but effective budgeting tool really works well. Also, with the help of this tool, I was able to make timely monthly payments towards my mountain load of debt (over $70,000), without ever being late on a payment! The best part about making payments on time is that you never have to worry about late payment fees. I still use the Monthly Bill Payment Schedule tool today, as it has proven to be an excellent way for me to manage my monthly bills. The Monthly Bill Payment Schedule was an effective tool for me during my debt repayment journey, and I believe it will work just as well for you!

NEEDS AND WANTS

There are many people who do not know the difference between a "need" and a "want" and consequently find themselves going over budget each month, due to this lack of knowledge. People are emotional spenders, and unless you have mastered the skill of being a conscious consumer, or you are living a minimalist lifestyle, you have most likely purchased items based on your emotional triggers — things that drive you to spend money such as "retail therapy," "panic buys" and "shoppers high." Knowing the difference between "needs" and "wants" will allow you to recognize your emotional trigger points when it comes to spending money. A "need" is something that is required to survive, like food, shelter and clothing. While it is not possible to skip your needs, it is possible to reduce the costs of your needs. A "want" is something that you desire to have, a nice luxury item that you have probably become accustomed to living with over the years. Unfortunately, these luxury items have negatively impacted your ability to have a balanced budget.

A need is something that is required for your survival that you cannot live without, and a want is something that you desire to have that you can live without.

As mentioned previously, you need to cut or trim any expenses that are creating a deficit in your budget, and that are not "needs" on your budget spreadsheet. Most fixed expenses fall under the "needs" category, and most variable expenses fall under the "wants" category. It is much easier to cut or trim items that are classified as "wants" than it is to cut or trim items that that are classified as "needs." In fact, there is currently a minimalist movement that is gaining a lot of traction whereby people are cutting out their "wants" by going on week long, month long, and even year long shopping bans, whereby they only spend money on their "needs." (Popular blogger Cait Flanders wrote a book about her year-long shopping ban in the book *The Year of Less*.) There is also a trend whereby people are moving into tiny homes to live a simplified life.

While I don't expect anyone to feel pressured to completely eliminate all their "wants," I do expect that some of the items that you are currently spending in the "wants" category will need to be either trimmed or cut out entirely. For example, if you have a gym membership that is costing you $50 per month, and you are currently heavily in debt, you need to cancel the gym membership. Instead, invest in a great pair of runners and begin exercising at home by watching free exercise videos that are available on platforms such as YouTube, take up running outdoors, use a skipping rope to stay in shape, or start going for daily power walks. By simply changing the way you choose to stay in shape, in the above example, you will save $600.00 a year. When I say "needs" versus "wants," this is what I mean:

TABLE 7. **NEEDS VS. WANTS**

Needs	Wants
Rent/Mortgage	Travel/Vacations
Utilities (heat, electricity, water, internet)	Cable
Home & Auto Insurance	RV/Trailer Insurance
Work Clothes	Designer Fashions
Groceries	Take-out/Restaurant Dining
Toiletries and Cleaning Supplies	Cleaning Service
Library Membership	Movie/Concert Tickets, Social events
Running Shoes	Gym Membership
Car Payment	Second Car Payment (You can't afford two car payments when you're in debt.)
Car Maintenance	Luxury Car Maintenance (You can't afford a luxury car when you're in debt. Downsize to a less expensive vehicle.)
Phone (smartphone with standard plan/ landline)	High Priced Smartphone with Expensive Data Plan
Public Transportation (Bus/Train)	Monthly Parking Fees/Toll Fees
Gas	Premium Gas (If you drive a car that needs premium gas, you are driving a luxury car, and you need to sell it ASAP and replace it with a less expensive car.)
Childcare/Daycare	Children's Extracurricular Sport Activities
Debt Repayment	Discretionary Spending (i.e. daily latte, buying designer shoes or sports equipment)

Since there is a huge psychological component to all debt repayment programs, continue paying for one of the items that falls under the "wants" category. This will help to keep you motivated during your SDRP journey. Each one of us deserves at least one item that brings us joy, even during the debt repayment process. For example, if you absolutely love drinking Starbucks coffee once or twice a day, and feel nauseous at the idea of having to give it up, then don't give it up. Allocate funds in your monthly budget for your daily latte and cut back on any expense that does not bring you the same level of joy.

Creating a monthly budget helps you stay on track and allows you to become more aware of where your monthly outflows and inflows are coming from; it's your ultimate tool to getting and staying out of debt. Your monthly budget will help you become a better money manager, and will guide you through your journey to becoming debt free. The goal is for you to have a balanced budget and to start controlling your money versus your money controlling you.

When you have a balanced budget you start controlling your money versus your money controlling you.

TABLE 8. **SAMPLE BALANCED BUDGET**

Sample budget: $3,000 monthly take-home pay

- Rent and utilities: $1,200
- Food: $450
- Auto/Transportation: $450
- Personal expenses: $350
- Credit card/College loan: $250
- Insurance: $200
- **LEFT OVER: $100**

Source: Merrill Lynch Wealth Management, "Debt and Retirement Savings" article (2014)

Your budget is going to include many line items that are specific to you. Here are examples of some monthly fixed and variable expenses, which have been categorized as either "Needs" or "Wants."

Needs

- Rent/Mortgage payment
- Groceries
- Car loan payment (One vehicle only)
- Car Insurance
- Public Transportation
- Home Insurance / Renters Insurance
- Property Taxes
- Childcare
- Condo Fees
- Internet
- Car License / Registration
- Life Insurance
- Health Insurance Premiums
- Utilities
- Car Repairs
- Gas
- Toiletries
- Home Phone

Wants

- Take Out and Restaurants (i.e. Coffee/Lattes, fast food, fine dining, snacks etc.)
- Entertainment

- Cable
- Cell Phone
- Pets
- Vacations
- Bank Fees
- Gifts
- Membership Fees
- Charity
- Hobbies and Interests
- Sports Fees
- Personal Care / Grooming
- Spending Money/Allowance

MAXIMIZING YOUR DEBT REPAYMENT PROGRAM

Here are a few ideas on how to turbocharge your SDRP program, and find even more money to pay off your debt faster:

- **Live on 50 Percent of Your Income:** The idea behind this strategy is for you to split your income—50% goes to pay your day-to-day necessities and 50% goes to paying your debts. If you are married or live in a common law relationship I encourage you to live on one income, and use the second income to pay off your debt. That is what my husband and I did when we implemented the Supercharged Financial Strategy. According to experts like Elizabeth Warren, Harvard Law School Professor who is now a US Senator, a person who is unable to live on half their income, is living beyond their means. If living on

50% of your income is not possible at the present time, then I want you to work your way up to living on 50% of your income. Start off with 20%, 30% or 40%, then work your way up to living on 50% of your income. You can also stress test this method by living on one income for the next six months, and see if it is something that works for you and your family. You will be amazed at how quickly you adjust to the 50% income strategy, as you see your debt melt away.

- **Get Rid of Overdraft Protection:** If you have overdraft protection on your checking account at your bank, get rid of it. This is just another way that you can get further into debt. The plan is to start managing your money in such a way that you will never have to rely on credit again.

- **Stop All Forms of Unplanned Shopping:** Stop all unplanned or impulse buying on groceries, clothes, electronics, vacations and even toiletries. Basically, stop all forms of unplanned shopping. Make a commitment to begin planning your shopping trips, this will add more money to your bottom line. Further to stopping unplanned shopping, bring a list with you on all planned grocery shopping and clothes shopping trips. Stick to the list and DO NOT digress from the list, no matter how good the sales are and how much you think that you'll be "saving" on whatever it is that is tempting you. Also, you want to seriously consider "unsubscribing" from all the online retailers that send you "deals" to your inbox. As mentioned previously, you need to learn all your emotional spending triggers so you can start spending less.

- **Use Cash:** Start using cash for all your discretionary daily expenditures. Since you have already stopped using your credit cards as part of the SDRP strategy, this step challenges you to stop using your debit cards (including Visa checking cards) and switch to using cash instead. Many people will find it challenging to switch to cash in our electronic world; however, I highly recommend that you try it for at least one month to see if this approach works for you. Start by using the cash envelope system whereby you fill envelopes, which represent the various categories of your variable expenses, with cash each payday. For example, if you have budgeted $400 for groceries in any given month, you would deposit $200 into your grocery envelope, and this amount would be used to purchase groceries over the next two weeks, until your next payday. If you find that this approach does not work for you after giving it a try, then you can switch back to using your debit cards for your everyday spending needs. You will see a noticeable improvement in your spending habits once you switch to cash. A study that was published in the Journal of Consumer Research found that people who use cash experience an emotional pain when they have to part with their money versus people who use credit cards. The credit card users are unconsciously willing to spend more, which has the unintended consequence of leaving less money to put to your debt payments. One final benefit of using cash is that once it's gone, you can't spend any more money.

- **Sell Your Vehicle:** If you currently have two vehicles, and at least one of those vehicles has equity in it, I want you to sell the equity rich vehicle and use the proceeds to pay down your debt. This is a strategy that I implemented during my SDRP journey, and it really served to help me tackle a great number of the debts listed on my SDRP Schedule.

CHAPTER 5

STEP 5: Add Extra Money to the Debt With the Smallest Balance

If you change the way you look at things, the things you look at change.

—WAYNE DYER

While I have already discussed the importance of putting windfall money towards your debt repayment in Step 3, I am kicking it up a couple of notches in Step 5. I now want you to apply extra money that you are going to receive by implementing all the money saving tools that I show you, towards your debt with the smallest balance. This is where you start seeing the full effects of the SDRP Strategy!

Now that you have reduced your monthly expenses and created a budget, and have applied windfall money towards the debt with the smallest balance, it is now time to find money in your budget that will allow you to permanently increase the minimum monthly payment on the debt with the smallest balance. I cannot emphasize enough just how important this step is in the SDRP process. This is where the "Supercharged" component of the SDRP strategy takes shape. Taking this one simple step will ensure that you pay off your debt faster than you would have if you only paid the minimum payment on your debt with the lowest balance. The key is that you will continue to make only the minimum payments on all your debts, except for the debt with the smallest balance. As discussed, the extra money that you'll be applying towards the smallest debt is money that you have carved out by implementing all the cost cutting tips that I have outlined for you.

When you keep applying extra money towards the debt with the smallest balance, you'll be overjoyed at how quickly your liabilities get paid off. Once the smallest debt is paid off then you need to apply the pyramid rule to the next following debt. The pyramid rule is when you take the payment that you were making on the recently paid off debt and apply it towards the next debt on your list. This pyramid rule accelerates the reduction of your remaining debt. Once you have fully paid off the first debt on your list, here is a breakdown of the payments that will be applied to the next smallest balance debt on your list:

1. The original pre-determined minimum payment for this debt,

2. The minimum payment from the debt that was just paid off,

3. Any additional money that you come across (i.e. work bonus, tax refund, birthday money).

As you can imagine, these steps will supercharge your debt repayment and you will be absolutely amazed at how quickly you pay off your debts from this point forward. By following Step 5 in the SDRP program, you will ensure that your entire debt is paid off in record time.

> **The 'Pyramid Rule' is when you take the payment that you were making on the recently paid off debt and apply it towards the next debt on your list.**

Keep following these payment instructions until all of your debt is paid in full. Here are some additional tips to free up cash in your budget so you can apply it towards the debt with the smallest balance.

HOW TO FREE UP CASH

There are so many ways you can free up cash and supercharge your SDRP program. Here are a few suggestions on how to free up cash so you can crush your debt faster:

* **Dump Your Bank Fees:** You can eliminate bank fees by opening a no-fee bank account. These accounts can be found at non-bricks and mortar banks, where you do all your banking online. Simplii Financial (Canada), Ally Bank (US), and TSB Bank

(UK) are a few examples of online banks. Research online to compare the services for the no-fee bank most accessible to you. This simple step can save you hundreds of dollars a year in bank fees.

- **Brew Your Own Coffee:** Bring your coffee or tea to work as opposed to buying it at your favourite coffee shop. You don't have to go cold turkey, but you can begin by buying your favourite coffee beans and brewing your coffee at home. This one move can save you a lot of money. If you spend $4 a day on your favourite coffee, and make two trips a day, this would cost you hundreds of dollars a year. You could cut your costs significantly by brewing your own coffee at home.

- **Quit Smoking:** If you smoke, quit smoking. Get help from a health professional who can provide guidance on the various smoking cessation programs available. This step alone can save you thousands of dollars a year. In one recent case I encountered, a chain smoker was spending $300 a month on cigarettes, which means he could be trimming $3600 a year from his budget by quitting this expensive habit.

- **Participate In A "Spend Free" Month:** Go for an entire month without spending money on anything except your basic "needs," such as food and shelter.

- **Eat In:** If you find that you are eating out most of the time, stop that! Start preparing meals at home, and only eat out once a week at the most. Also, prepare larger portions of food at home so there are leftovers that you can pack as your lunch for work. This single act will save you thousands of dollars a year. There are great online resources that can help you begin planning meals at home.

- **Stop Buying Lottery Tickets:** Stop buying lottery tickets and start applying the money you spend on them to your debt repayment plan. Every penny counts when it comes to getting out of debt, and the $5–$10 that you currently spend weekly on lottery tickets is keeping you further in debt.

- **Curb Your Entertainment Spending:** If you go to the movie theatre regularly then you need to cut this out of your budget. Look into subscribing to a monthly movie streaming service like Netflix, which will set you back only about $11 a month. By the time you pay for tickets, popcorn and drinks at the movie theater, you have easily spent $25 to $30 per person.

- **Get the Best Deals on Cable and the Internet:** You may have to cut your cable and start watching programs on-line or through a streaming service such as Netflix. Your data usage will go up so shop around for the best internet deals.

- **Watch Your Cell Phone Usage:** As mentioned previously, review your cell phone bill and find ways to reduce your monthly fees by choosing a less expensive plan.

- **Stay Fit:** You may need to cut your gym membership out of your budget. You can buy a great pair of runners, and take up running, or speed walking.

There are a lot of great workout videos available at your local library that you can borrow for free!

- **Reduce Your Alcohol Consumption:** If you like to drink alcohol regularly, you could reduce your consumption and use the extra money to pay down your debts.

- **Cancel Magazine and Other Subscriptions:** Cut subscriptions to magazines newspapers, and any other services that you are currently subscribed to. Instead, start going online for your information and news; not only is it current, it's free!

- **Take Personal Grooming Into Your Own Hands:** If you like to get manicures and pedicures, you should start doing your nails at home. If you are good at cutting hair, you may have to start trimming your hair at home. If you are horrified at the prospects of cutting your own hair, you can enlist the help of family or friends who are hairstylists. You can also go one step further by requesting a free hair cut in exchange for cutting someone's grass or helping them out with some other home maintenance or repair project.

Now that you have applied extra money towards your debt with the smallest balance, it's time to build your emergency fund.

CHAPTER 6

STEP 6: Build an Emergency Fund

**The art is not in making money,
but in keeping it.**

—PROVERB

To prevent yourself from falling back into a financial hole, you need to build an emergency fund. You must start building your emergency fund at the same time as you are repaying your debt. The main reason that people get into debt is because they have not planned for the unexpected events that show up in life — a sudden job loss, emergency car repair, an increase in annual insurance premiums, an unexpected medical expense —just to name a few. These unexpected events are actually more common than you realize. Therefore, it is really important to plan for them.

While it is virtually impossible to know what life will

throw your way, it is absolutely possible, and imperative, to plan for the unexpected events in life. Not only
will you be less stressed when an unexpected financial
emergency pops up, you will have the financial resources
to take care of that emergency. Setting aside money to
handle life's emergencies is one of the secrets to living
a financially abundant life. I imagine being laid off in
my twenties would have been a lot less stressful had I
built up a healthy emergency fund. Accordingly, you need
to plan for these unexpected emergencies by regularly
setting aside money in an emergency fund.

Many financial advisors recommend that you save
three to six months of expenses in your emergency fund.
However, I take it one step further and recommend that
you save eight to twelve months of expenses in your
emergency fund. My recommended savings target might
sound crazy, and may also be daunting, but trust me
when I say that it will be much easier to achieve this
savings target once you have implemented all the steps
that I have laid out for you in the SDRP program. You
will be amazed at how much money you will have to
put towards your emergency fund. By simply following
the Supercharged Financial Strategy all the financial
"fat" that was once weighing you down will melt away,
which will result in you saving a lot of money.

Building your emergency fund is an extremely
important step in the SDRP program. Failure to build
an emergency fund may result in you falling back into
old debt habits, such as reaching for a credit card when
unplanned life events present themselves.

Having an emergency fund will allow you to prosper
during times of financial upheaval. One of the primary

reasons people don't achieve their financial goals is because they fail to have an emergency fund. Here are some examples of real life events that may qualify as unexpected emergencies:

- Your car breaks down and requires emergency repair;

- Your furnace motor blows out during the middle of winter;

- You unexpectedly lose your job, and it takes you several months to find new employment;

- Your roof starts leaking and you are required to install new shingles;

- Your garage door opener motor breaks down, and you need to replace it;

- Your stove stops working, your dishwasher motor blows out, or your freezer stops running and needs to either be repaired or replaced;

- You get into a serious accident, which results in your being injured, and you are required to stay home for more than three months. If you are a contract worker, you're out of income for more than three months; however, if you are employed with a corporation that has disability benefits you soon realize that you are only covered for 60% of your wages, and need to use your emergency fund to cover some of your monthly expenses.

These scenarios are only a few examples of the emergencies that can pop up in life. An entire book could be written on all the different types of emergencies that life throws you. I have experienced each one of the above referenced emergencies in my own life, so the list reflects real life emergencies. Whatever the emergency, you want to make sure that you have a plan of action in place to deal with it. My emergency fund has come to my rescue many times. In fact, having an emergency fund in place allowed me to transition smoothly from full-time employee to full-time entrepreneur. The most important detail of the emergency fund is that you need to save eight to twelve months of your living expenses in that fund. It really is a matter of when these life events occur, and not if they will occur. Saving money in an emergency fund gives you the peace of mind that you'll never again have to go back into debt to deal with any financial situation.

> **The most important detail of the emergency fund is that you need to save eight to twelve months of your living expenses in that fund.**

I can personally attest to the fact that having an emergency fund serves to boost your financial confidence, and allows you to face any financial hurdle with a sense of awareness and power. I am confident that you will be able to handle any financial hurdle you encounter with confidence and a sense of empowerment!

Before we get into the details of the steps required to implement your emergency fund savings, it is important to list those life events that do not qualify as emergencies.

EVENTS THAT DO NOT WARRANT DIPPING INTO YOUR EMERGENCY FUND:

- Your best friend is getting married in a tropical location and has asked you to be part of the wedding ceremony, and requested that you pay for your own travel and accommodations. This is not an emergency, and you should not be dipping into your emergency savings to fund this venture.

- On your way home from work you stop off at Costco to pick up some groceries and notice a beautiful living room set that has recently been marked down. Unless you are in dire need of new furniture, this would not qualify as an emergency.

- A group of your friends have invited you to attend the concert of a legendary band, and the tickets cost over $200 each—this does not qualify as an emergency. If you are in debt, and if you have not saved for these tickets in advance, you cannot afford to purchase a ticket.

- You have been asked to pitch in to buy an expensive wedding/anniversary gift for a family member, and you feel pressured into contributing to the group gift. Although it is difficult to say "no" to your family, this is not an emergency, and the right thing to do is to say "no" to your family. This is an opportunity for you to be honest and tell your loved ones that you cannot afford to contribute to the gift because you're in debt.

- A colleague from work invites you and a few other co-workers out for dinner after work; you really like the group of people attending the gathering and want to join them for dinner and cocktails, so you consider taking money out of your emergency fund to attend the event. DON'T DO IT! This is definitely not an emergency, and does not warrant you making a withdrawal from your emergency fund.

STEPS TO BUILDING AN EMERGENCY FUND

- Open up a separate "no-fee" high interest savings account at a bank of your choice (If you open the account at a non-bricks and mortar bank like Ally Financial, in the U.S., or Simplii Financial, in Canada, you will save hundreds of dollars a year in fees).

- Begin by setting aside ten to fifteen percent of your net take-home pay each time you get paid and deposit the money into your newly created high interest savings account. The high interest savings account is now considered your emergency fund. For maximum success, the predetermined emergency fund amount must be automatically transferred to your emergency fund each payday from the account where your paycheque is deposited.

- Make sure that your high interest savings account is not linked to your debit card. This ensures that you are either forced to physically go into a bank to withdraw the money, or, if the account is at a virtual online bank, then you will need to make the transfer online, which usually takes two business days to clear. You want your emergency fund money to be hard to access, thereby ensuring that the money is not being used for non-emergency day-to-day expenses.

- The high interest account that you open to serve as your emergency fund must be highly liquid and should not be linked to an investment brokerage account that is capable of trading in stocks, bonds, ETFs (Exchange Traded Funds), or mutual funds. The money allotted to your emergency fund should never be invested in individual stocks, bonds, mutual funds or ETFs. It is too risky to invest money from your emergency fund into the stock market. Money in your emergency fund should be saved in a guaranteed savings account that is highly liquid, safe, and accessible within a reasonable period of time in the event of an emergency (within 1-2 business days). Money invested in the stock market is subject to volatility, and there is no room for volatility when it comes to your emergency fund.

- Don't worry about not having the financial resources required to fund your emergency account. You will have the money required for your emergency fund once you have implemented all the previous steps that I have outlined in the SDRP program. Step 4 of the SDRP program provided details of what actions you need to take to create your budget, and provided information related to finding extra money in your budget. The extra money you find in your budget will be the source of funding your SDRP and emergency fund. Creating your budget will give you a clear picture of how much money you can comfortably contribute to your emergency fund each month. I know this might sound difficult to complete, but it will not be as hard to do once you get your SDRP program underway. Having a savings goal of ten to fifteen percent will ensure that you reach your eight to twelve month emergency fund target within a reasonable period of time. You owe it to yourself to make this a priority.

- View your emergency fund as a bill that needs to be paid each payday. Make it a top priority, right up there with your rent or mortgage payment. Add your emergency fund payment as a bill on your Monthly Bill Payment Schedule.

- Finally, I cannot emphasize enough the importance of automating your monthly emergency fund contributions. This one step will be the most important thing you do as it relates to your emergency fund. You are increasing your odds of successfully achieving your goal of saving eight to twelve months of your monthly expenses.

- Make sure to invest in a safe vehicle like a high interest savings account at either a traditional bricks and mortar bank or a non-traditional online bank that is insured by the federal regulatory body in your jurisdiction (i.e. Canadian Deposit Insurance Corporation or CDIC in Canada and the Federal Deposit Insurance Corporation or FDIC in the US).

- Resist the temptation of using the money in your emergency fund for any other purpose than emergencies. Using your emergency fund as a spending account will derail your chances of getting out of debt. Having an emergency fund is an essential part of the SDRP program, which serves to eliminate the likelihood of you having to reach for a credit card or line of credit each time an emergency presents itself. Whatever you do, DO NOT use a line of credit as an emergency fund, because you will simply get back into debt. Remember that when you began your SDRP journey you made a commitment to accumulate NO NEW DEBT! Consider the emergency fund as a security blanket that allows you to sleep soundly each night.

Once you have built your emergency fund you will be amazed at how much more confident you feel about your financial life. You'll begin to feel a sense of control over your finances as opposed to your finances controlling you. Your financial awareness will be greater as you set your intentions to pay off your debt and become financially free.

> **Once you build your emergency fund you'll begin to feel a sense of control over your finances as opposed to your finances controlling you.**

While you're paying off your debt, your emergency fund will be in place to take care of the unexpected events that arise in life, and you will be able to handle whatever event life throws at you. Gone are the days of reaching for your credit card when unplanned things happen, because you have taken the initiative to plan for the "what ifs" in life. You now have the protection of an emergency fund that allows you to stay on course and on target as it relates to achieving your debt repayment goals.

CHAPTER 7

STEP 7: Maintain Your Newfound Debt Free Status and Implement SWAP Strategy

Growth is the great separator between those who succeed and those who do not. When I see a person beginning to separate themselves from the pack, it's almost always due to personal growth.

—JOHN C. MAXWELL

Once you have completed all the previous steps, and have consistently made monthly payments on your debt, you will soon approach the day when you make your last payment. I can tell you from my own experience that you will feel absolutely fantastic on that monumental day. You will have accomplished a goal that seemed insurmountable when you first began your journey. And this accomplishment will give you the motivation to continue a debt free existence. Once you attain this level of financial freedom you may be wondering how you can maintain your newfound debt free status, and how you are going to turn the SDRP strategy into the SWAP strategy. Here are some straightforward tips on how to maintain your new debt free status.

MAINTAINING A DEBT FREE LIFE

Let's begin by looking at the things you need to do to maintain your new debt free status. These are all things I did once I paid off over $70,000 of consumer debt:

- Live on a cash-based system—pay all your variable expenses (groceries, gas, entertainment etc.) with cash, or cash equivalents (debit cards).

- When you are tempted to use your credit card on a transaction, ask yourself these three questions: 1) "Do I really need this item?" 2) "Will I be able to pay this item off at the end of the month?" 3) "Do I absolutely have to buy this item right now?" If you are able to answer "Yes" to all three questions, then you can proceed with your purchase. However, whenever possible avoid using your credit card for any purchase, and opt instead to use either cash or your debit card. If you are unable to answer "Yes" to the previous questions, then don't buy the item. It's in your best interest to wait until you have the financial means to buy the item. The last thing you want is to get back into debt.

- Share your debt repayment story with anyone who will listen, especially close family and friends. You want to ensure that those closest to you are aware of the struggles and victories that you've been through, so they are less inclined to sabotage your newfound debt free status, and more inclined to learn about how you managed to become financially secure. You'll be surprised by how many family and friends will begin asking you how they too can get out of debt!

- Begin surrounding yourself with like-minded people who are financially aware, and are on their path to being financially independent, or who have already reached financial independence. It is a lot easier to live a debt free life if you surround yourself with people who understand your motivation and are supportive of the life-changing decisions you have made. If you encounter any family or friends who are unsupportive of your debt free lifestyle, make sure to steer clear of them as much as possible. Stay away from people who are spendthrifts. The last thing you want is to surround yourself with people who you know like to spend a lot of money, and more importantly, who you know can influence you to get back into debt. Just as a recovering alcoholic is advised to stay away from friends and associates who encourage them to drink, you need to keep your distance from family, friends and associates who encourage you to get back into debt. You have made the incredible decision to become financially free, and it's not uncommon to encounter loved ones who knowingly or unknowingly do things that can potentially hinder your progress. You have transformed your money mindset, and subsequently have tapped into your true self. Your loved ones may not recognize this version of you, and may be fearful of losing the old you. It is up to you to keep moving forward on your road to success. If you have friends or family members who are heavily in debt and are looking for ways to attain financial freedom, then by all means, recommend this book to them and help steer them towards the path to financial freedom.

You will be able to maintain your new debt free status by simply following these tips. I know that you will be successful in your debt repayment journey as long as you stick to the SDRP program.

SWAP PROGRAM

At the beginning of the book I promised to cover the SWAP strategy for you to turn your debt repayment strategy into a wealth creation strategy. Here is a breakdown of the Supercharged Wealth Accumulation Plan, which is to be implemented as soon as you complete the SDRP program.

The Supercharged Wealth Accumulation Plan (SWAP) is a system that I used to build great wealth once I finished paying off my debt. It is a simple plan and requires just one important thing—the willingness to keep applying all your monthly SDRP payments towards the newly designated SWAP payments. Since you have gone for months, and possibly even years, without spending these funds on discretionary items, you will not be making any more sacrifices than you have already made under the SDRP program.

Once you make your final SDRP payment, I want you to begin applying the entire monthly SDRP payment towards your new SWAP payment—the funds will be deposited into a high interest savings account. This high interest savings account is not to be confused with the high interest savings account that you previously opened when you set up your emergency fund. Instead, you will open a new high-interest savings account whereby you will deposit the newly designated SWAP payments each and every month.

The SWAP account is to be opened as soon as you have made your last SDRP payment. Then you are to automate the savings to ensure that the funds make their way to your SWAP account. I cannot emphasize enough just how important it is for you to automate your monthly SWAP payments. By automating the payments you ensure that the funds will make their way to the rightful place and you avoid the temptation of spending this money on other items.

SET A GOAL

At this stage of the wealth accumulation process you will have spent months, if not years, paying off your debt, and it would certainly be tempting to take the money that you were previously paying towards your SDRP and use it to splurge on a fabulous trip, or some consumer product. I know just how tempting it is to use the money for discretionary consumer products, but I'm here to assure you that it's in your best interest to use the funds to create true lasting wealth that will change your life forever. Once I made my last SDRP payment I was very tempted to take the new money and splurge on brand new clothes and furniture for my home. However, there was something liberating in knowing that I could take my wealth to the next level by setting up the SWAP program, which would allow me to build my wealth and create more opportunities for myself and my family.

I began to dream about all the possibilities and options that I would be afforded by committing to this wealth accumulation system, and came up with the following goal: I decided that I would pay off my mortgage within ten years of starting the SWAP program. I am very happy to report that while it ended up taking me closer to twelve years to pay off, I was able to accomplish my goal, and my husband and I are now living mortgage free. I share this story to show you what is possible when you make the commitment to convert the SDRP strategy into the SWAP strategy. Your SWAP payments are what will catapult you to the next level of financial freedom. In fact, I called my SWAP account my "dream account."

The SWAP strategy is to be used to build your financial safety net and your wealth, and will allow you to make sound investments so you can realize your dreams —hence the term "dream account." The goal is to have enough money saved up in your SWAP account to enable you to fund all your investment accounts (Roth IRA, Tax Free Savings Account, Individual Savings Account, Registered Retirement Savings Plan, Non-Registered Investment accounts, Children's education plans such as Registered Education Savings Plan's and 529 College Plans, or any other type of investment account), to buy cash flowing real estate investments, to invest in your business, or simply to invest in yourself. The best part is that you can choose how to allocate the money in the SWAP account to build your wealth. In addition to using the funds in my SWAP account to pay off my mortgage, I also used the funds to buy real estate properties, buy individual stocks, and to invest in my business. I was able to attain a seven figure net worth as a result of all my investment opportunities.

Since you have already become accustomed to living within your means, you will not miss the SDRP payments that you are now redirecting towards your SWAP account. In fact, you will begin to feel confident in your financial future, and will most likely find additional funds to put towards your SWAP account.

The SWAP account also serves the purpose of acting like a contingency account (also known as a sinking fund), because it allows you to deposit money in the account with the objective of using it to fund an expense that will come up sometime in the foreseeable future. For example, I have deposited funds in my SWAP account that were subsequently used to purchase vehicles, to pay cash for my vacations, and to buy new appliances. It is absolutely amazing to use cash for the purchase of big ticket items. I can't wait for you to do the same!

The SWAP account also acts like a contingency account or sinking fund, because it allows you to fund expenses that are anticipated to come up in the foreseeable future.

The SWAP strategy will change your life, as it has changed mine, and it will provide you and your family with the financial safety net that you previously only dreamed about. I recommend that you continue saving your money in the SWAP account indefinitely, and begin to get comfortable with saving at least 50% of your income in your SWAP account.

There is no better feeling in this world than when you have your financial house in order and you no longer feel shackled by the weight of debt. Getting rid of debt is the most crucial thing you need to do to take control of your financial destiny, and adding the SWAP strategy to the mix is the most crucial thing you need to do to build life changing wealth. The Supercharged Financial Strategy will allow you to create a financial future that is truly brighter and a whole lot lighter. You can do it! If you have gone out of your way to purchase this book, it means you are serious about your financial future, and I'm confident that you have what it takes to get out of debt, stay out of debt, and create great wealth too!

For me personally, building wealth was predicated on my ability to shift my mindset from a scarcity model to an abundance model. I started believing that I was deserving of wealth, and there was an abundance of wealth to be had. It was not about having more stuff, but instead was about having more options. When you implement the SWAP strategy you open yourself up to so many great wealth building opportunities. Building wealth has indeed provided me with more options to live my best possible life.

CHAPTER 8

Other Debt Management Options

Beware of little expenses. A small
leak will sink a great ship.

—BENJAMIN FRANKLIN

At the beginning of the book I promised to discuss additional options that are available to you for getting out of debt. This is a bonus chapter that focuses on other debt management options besides the Supercharged Debt Repayment Plan. If you have taken all the necessary steps in the SDRP program, and you are still finding it difficult to fund your debt repayment, then it's time to look into these other debt management options.

OPTION 1. DEBT SETTLEMENT

The debt settlement option is most effective when you find yourself a few months behind on your debt payments.

However, you can't be more than six months behind on your payments for this option to work. If you are, your lender will most likely send your outstanding debt to a collection agency, and at this stage it is too late to try to settle your debt directly with your lender. The debt settlement option should only be used once you have exhausted all other possible options for getting out of debt, including the SDRP option, and, you are finding it nearly impossible to pay back your debt.

This option is typically used for those who are struggling with a lot of credit card debt, as opposed to other types of debt. Also, with the debt settlement option, you have to be behind on your payments before you can settle with the lender. Once you are behind on a few payments you will most likely receive either a call or a notification letter from your lender requesting that you bring your payments up-to-date. Do not ignore the phone call or notification letter from the lender. Take this opportunity to reach out to your lender, contact them to make a settlement arrangement. Your lender will be more inclined to work with you when you contact them as soon as possible, as opposed to waiting until the lender contacts you.

A debt settlement arrangement typically involves you offering to pay your lender a certain percentage of your outstanding debt as payment in full for that debt. For example, if you owe $10,000 of credit card debt you can offer to pay 30% of that outstanding debt as payment in full. Therefore, you would be offering to give the lender $3000 to settle the debt in full. Your lender will most likely reject this initial offer, and come back with a counteroffer that is closer to 50% to 60% of the outstanding balance. If you are able to come up with 50% to 60% of your current outstanding debt balance, then you're in a great position to offer a debt settlement arrangement to your lenders. Accordingly, in this example, you would have to come up with $5000–$6000 to settle your debt with the lender.

However, if you do not currently have the funds available to make a lump sum payment on your debt, which is likely the case for many people, then you can also negotiate a monthly payment with your lender. Under this arrangement you would agree to pay a percentage of the agreed-upon amount in full, and would proceed to make monthly payments directly to your lender for a pre-set number of months, until the debt is paid in full. It is important to note that negotiating a debt settlement with your lenders most likely will result in your credit score being negatively impacted. However, this is a small price to pay in order to pay off your debt!

OPTION 2. DEBT MANAGEMENT PROGRAM AND CONSUMER PROPOSALS

With this option you would contact a reputable credit counselling service in your area, and discuss options with them such as a debt management program (also known as a personalized plan) or a consumer proposal. I would highly caution people from using any debt settlement service that is offered by a for-profit organization. In North America, these for-profit companies usually charge anywhere between $1500 and $3000 for the same service offered at a non-profit consumer credit counselling agency for a nominal cost. Here is the contact information for some consumer credit counselling agencies located in various parts of the world:

- Canada—www.creditcounsellingcanada.ca. The industry is not highly regulated in Canada. When you go to the website make sure to click on the province that you live in to get in touch with a non-profit counsellor located near you;

- United States—www.nfcc.org (National Foundation for Credit Counseling), and www.fcaa.org (Financial Counseling Association of America). Both of these organizations are centrally regulated and have locations throughout the United States. Go to either one of these organizations to contact a non-profit credit counselling agency located near you;

- The United Kingdom—www.stepchange.org. This agency was previously called Consumer Credit Counselling Services, but is now called StepChange Debt Charity, and they have authorization from the Financial Conduct Authority to administer debt settlements, among other services;

- European Union—www.sfz.uni-mainz.de/2626.php is a site you can visit to get the direct contact information for various debt management agencies located in different countries in the European Union. Click on the link to the country you live in, and contact the respective credit counselling organizations located near you.

Debt Management Program

Under a debt management program the credit counselling service proposes to amalgamate all your unsecured debt payments into one monthly payment. With this option you pay the entire balance owing on your debt, and, unlike the debt settlement option, you are unable to negotiate a partial payment arrangement under this program.

Furthermore, the interest charges on your debt are either reduced or eliminated under this option. It's important to note that you will only be offered the debt management plan, or a personalized plan, as it is known in the United States, if all your lenders agree to the arrangement. If even one of your lenders does not agree with the arrangement, you can't proceed with a debt management program.

There are fees associated with setting up a debt management program. In North America, there is a one-time set-up fee that is typically under $100 and a 10% administrative fee that is taken out of your monthly payments. The information pertaining to the debt management program stays on your credit report for a maximum of two years after your debt is paid off. One benefit of proceeding with a debt management program with a credit counselling agency is that you will be able to keep your assets (home and car), and will not be required to sell your assets to pay back your lenders.

I strongly believe that you need to keep a record of your debt management program in perpetuity, because it is the only proof you will ever have that the agreed upon arrangement was made. Also, upon completing your payments make sure to ask the credit counselling agency to write you a letter stating that all the required payments under the program have been made in full.

You will be able to provide this letter to any financial institution, employer or landlord that requests proof that you completed the program and made the full payment under the arrangement. Keeping great records of your debt management program will serve you well in the future!

Consumer Proposal

A consumer proposal is another option that a credit counselling service can make on your behalf. In North America the initial fees and costs associated with a consumer proposal are approximately $1500.

A consumer proposal is a legal process that needs to be administered by a Licensed Insolvency Trustee in Canada, and a bankruptcy attorney in the United States. In Canada, the Trustee retains up to 20% of all funds paid to your lenders under this arrangement. If you decide on this option to pay off your debt you're only required to pay a portion of the balance owing, and the term of the payment is typically three to four years in duration. While a consumer proposal is not considered bankruptcy proceedings, it is serious enough that the information stays on your credit report for three years after completing the payments. Be prepared to agree to make payments over the duration of the proposal, which can sometimes extend for several years, depending on your total outstanding debt.

OPTION 3. BANKRUPTCY

The third debt management option available to those who find themselves in a situation where their debt has ballooned to unmanageable levels is bankruptcy. The decision to file for bankruptcy should only be made after all other options have been exhausted—it's a decision of last resort. I am hard-pressed to believe that anyone would ever make the decision to file for bankruptcy lightly, and would caution those considering bankruptcy to do their best to exhaust all other options before deciding to file for bankruptcy.

If the debt that you owe is greater than the assets that you own then you might be a candidate for bankruptcy. For example, if you owe $100,000 of consumer debt, and you currently own $50,000 of assets, then you may have to seriously consider filing for bankruptcy.

Bankruptcy is a legal proceeding that must be administered by a Licensed Insolvency Trustee in Canada, or an attorney in the US. There are fees associated with filing for bankruptcy. In both Canada and the US the fees can set you back a couple of thousands of dollars or more, depending on your financial situation. The bankruptcy process begins with a petition filed by the debtor, and the assets that are owned by the debtor may be used to repay a portion of the outstanding debt. The bankruptcy process allows a person to discharge most of their debt. However, there are some debts that cannot be discharged in bankruptcy. For example, outstanding child support payments cannot be discharged in bankruptcy. Also, some student loans and outstanding income taxes cannot be discharged in bankruptcy. Each country has its own legal procedures and laws pertaining to bankruptcy, and it is imperative that you contact a bankruptcy professional in your respective jurisdiction for more information to determine if bankruptcy is a viable option for you.

Overall, the best course of action for you to take is to pay back all your lenders the entire amount that you owe them, one payment at a time. I am proof that the slow and steady approach works, and I truly believe that if I was able to pay off over $70,000 of consumer debt, you can pay off your debt too! Stick with the Supercharged Debt Repayment Plan and crush your liabilities for good!

CHAPTER 9

Wishing You Success

Begin, be bold, and venture to be wise.

−HORACE

PARTING THOUGHTS

Now that you have read this book and learned how to implement the SDRP and SWAP strategies, you need to put the plan into action. You will get out of debt with the SDRP strategy, and increase your wealth with the SWAP strategy. Your life will begin to change for the better the minute you implement the Supercharged Financial Strategy. You'll never again have to rely on credit to get by in your day-to-day life. Paying off your liabilities will increase your financial flexibility and allow you to live the life of your dreams. You'll have more options available to you because you'll no longer be enslaved by the burden of your debt. By implementing the SWAP strategy you can increase your net worth, and build a strong financial foundation that will allow you to make choices that serve your life's purpose.

You had the courage to admit that you needed help getting out of debt, you were able to shift your mindset to prepare yourself to successfully tackle your debt, and figured out why you are getting out of debt by establishing your Debt Motivation Statement. You exhibited the emotional fortitude required to actually get out of debt by implementing the 7 *Steps to Get Out of Debt and Build Wealth*.

Now that you have successfully addressed the physical, psychological and spiritual components of your finances, you are ready to take full control of your financial future and live the life of your dreams. Your commitment to getting out of debt has increased your financial awareness and helped you get closer to realizing your goals in life.

After implementing the SDRP and SWAP strategies in my own life, I was able to face the scariest financial events, with ease, grace and confidence. In fact, later on in my career when I encountered another layoff, I was not stressed out about this event at all. However, I should have been stressed out because I was three months pregnant when I was laid off the second time around. Instead of being stressed, I felt completely calm because I had taken all the necessary steps to secure my financial future. I had done the work to set myself up for financial success. I'm still amazed at how different the layoff experience was after having implemented the Supercharged Financial Strategy, versus the experience of being laid off in my twenties, when I was broke, scared and completely unprepared. The second time around, I was in control and empowered. The Supercharged Financial Strategy helps you shift your mindset and improve your financial circumstances.

You have now conquered your debt demons head on, and by doing so can live a life filled with peace and joy, and begin to pursue your passion in life. You're now living in alignment with your true self, and have given yourself the ultimate gift of being debt free and on the path to financial freedom.

I'm so proud of you for taking this important step to get out of debt and build your wealth, and can't wait to hear from you once you reach your financial goals. Please send me a direct message on any one of my social media accounts to share your financial milestones and success stories with me. I look forward to connecting with each of you! But, until such time, make sure to continue to Supercharge—Your—Life, and keep moving towards the realization of your dreams. I wish each one of you great success!

AFTERWORD

Getting out of over $390,000 of debt was a huge undertaking. There were many times throughout my journey that I wanted to give up, and just revert back to my old habits. However, I never gave up because I found ways to keep myself motivated and supercharged throughout my journey. One way that I stayed motivated was to read my Debt Motivation Statement on a daily basis. I also did one particular thing to stay motivated that was quite unconventional—I decided to keep all my old credit card, line of credit, student loan, and department store statements from the early days of my debt-repayment journey. For whatever reason, revisiting those old debt statements every now and then would give me the motivation I needed to stay focused and on track to achieve my financial goals.

Therefore, in the spirit of helping you stay motivated in your debt free journey, I'm sharing a before and after snapshot of some of my old debt statements from when I first embarked on my SDRP journey. You will see the before and after statements and invoices pertaining to my mortgage, credit cards, line of credit, and student loans. You'll also see a copy of an old ATM bank receipt that shows the overdrawn status of my chequing account. The sad irony of the ATM receipt is that the "money" that was being withdrawn from my chequing account was being used to make a Visa payment, and the Visa balance had already surpassed the credit limit. I have also attached an old Visa Statement for you to view, which has a balance of $5240.50. However, if you look closely, you'll notice that the credit limit on the Visa is $5000, which means that the Visa was over the limit by $240.50! There is no denying the seriousness of my financial situation at the time—I was withdrawing funds from an overdrawn account to pay an overdrawn bill! Ouch!

I hope that by sharing my personal debt snapshot you recognize that you are not alone, and more importantly, it will show you that you too can conquer your debt demons, just as I have conquered mine. I encourage you to complete your own before and after snapshot of your liabilities by taking all your original debt statements at the beginning of your journey, and comparing them with the final statement that is issued for each respective debt. I am confident that this one action will help keep you motivated, and on target as you embark on your wealth creation journey.

MORTGAGE DOCUMENTS—BEFORE

Statement of Adjustment

Purchaser: Adeola & Adam
Address:
Legal Description:
Possession Date: February 17, 2004

Selling price (exclude GST)		271,669.00
Schedule C - 1	240.00	
Schedule C - 2	4,470.00	
Schedule C - 3	(2.75)	
Schedule C - 4	n/c	
Schedule C - 5	5,372.40	
Schedule C - 6	2,702.00	
Schedule C - 7	n/c	
Schedule C - 7A	4,382.87	
Schedule C - 7B	1,617.50	
Schedule C - 7C	683.00	
Schedule C - 7D	6,079.91	
Schedule C - 7E	1,185.00	26,729.93
Total amounts before GST		298,398.93
Add: 7% GST		20,887.93
Less: GST Rebate (36%)		(7,519.65)
Total Net Selling Price (include GST)		311,767.20
Payment received by Landmark:		
Deposit received	10,000.00	
Deposit received	18,383.98	
Property Taxes ($ x /365)	Undetermined	
Association Fees ($214 x42/365)		24.62
(Portion of April 1 - March 31, 2004)		
Closing balance	283,407.84	
	311,791.82	311,791.82

Home Systems

Customer: ADAM & ADEOLA
Address:
Contact:
Job#

   Contact:

Location	Product Code	Description	Unit Price	Price
Multi-Room				
Kitchen	Pro-PL6C	8" Ceiling Speakers	1	$ 89.95
	Pro-vcidec	Volume Control	1	$ 29.95
Outdoor	Pre-w	Pre-wire/Speaker	1	$ 25.00
Theatre Room	CP-8	8" Tru-Audio Ceiling Speakers	1	$ 193.00
Master Bedroom	Pro-PL6C	6" Ceiling Speakers	1	$ 69.95
	Pro-vcidec	Volume Control	1	$ 29.95
Bedroom 2	Pre-w	Pre-wire/Speaker	1	$ 25.00
Bedroom 3	Pre-w	Pre-wire/Speaker	1	$ 25.00
Garage	Pro-PL6C	6" Ceiling Speakers	1	$ 69.95
	Pro-vcidec	Volume Control	1	$ 29.95
Theatre room	DV-6	Dual Coil 6.5" Speaker	1	$ 80.00
all equipment to be installed	Pro-vcidec	Volume Control	1	$ 29.95
	Shop/Suppl	Shop Supplies and Materials	1	$ 80.00
	TX-SR500	5.1 DTS Amplifier	1	$ 415.00
	DX-C380	CD Changer	1	$ 270.00
	DV-SP300	DVDPlayer	1	$ 300.00
	48211-6a	1x6 Passive Audio	1	$ 70.00
	JBL-Studiocen	Centre Channel	1	$ 320.00
	JBL-Studio38	Book Shelf	1	$ 538.00
	JBL-PB10	Powered Subwoofer	1	$ 400.00
		Total		$ 3,090.65
		GST (7%)		$ 216.34
		Grand Total		$ 3,306.99

Job Completion Form
Date Completed
Installer

STONETILE   INVOICE

03/02/04

ADAM

Original contract amount   4491.00

Gross billing to date   4491.00
Previous gross billing   0.00
On completion per contract   4,491.00
***Note:Deposit of $1200.00 applied on
account (see statement)***

                    GST   314.37
            PLEASE PAY THIS AMOUNT>   4,805.37

        PLEASE REMIT,AS PAYMENT IS DUE ON RECEIPT OF THIS INVOICE

MORTGAGE DOCUMENTS—AFTER

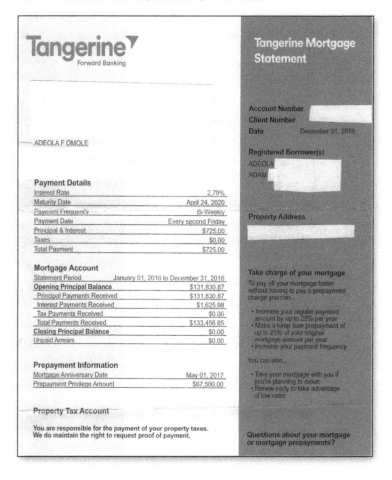

Tangerine
Forward Banking

Tangerine Mortgage Statement

Account Number
Client Number
Date   December 31, 2016

ADEOLA F OMOLE

Registered Borrower(s)
ADEOLA
ADAM

Payment Details

Interest Rate	2.79%
Maturity Date	April 24, 2020
Payment Frequency	Bi-Weekly
Payment Date	Every second Friday
Principal & Interest	$725.00
Taxes	$0.00
Total Payment	$725.00

Property Address

Mortgage Account

Statement Period	January 01, 2016 to December 31, 2016
Opening Principal Balance	$131,830.87
Principal Payments Received	$131,830.87
Interest Payments Received	$1,625.98
Tax Payments Received	$0.00
Total Payments Received	$133,456.85
Closing Principal Balance	$0.00
Unpaid Arrears	$0.00

Take charge of your mortgage

To pay off your mortgage faster without having to pay a prepayment charge you can...

- Increase your regular payment amount by up to 25% per year
- Make a lump sum prepayment of up to 25% of your original mortgage amount per year
- Increase your payment frequency

You can also...

- Take your mortgage with you if you're planning to move
- Renew early to take advantage of low rates

Prepayment Information

Mortgage Anniversary Date	May 01, 2017
Prepayment Privilege Amount	$67,500.00

Property Tax Account

You are responsible for the payment of your property taxes. We do maintain the right to request proof of payment.

Questions about your mortgage or mortgage prepayments?

CREDIT LINE—BEFORE

Royal Bank

RBC

Annual Statement

ADEOLA OMOLE

We thank you for your business and are pleased to advise you on the status of your loan.

Reporting Period from Jan 1, 2002 to Dec 31, 2002

DETAILS OF YOUR LOAN
Loan number: Loan type: ROYAL CREDIT LINE Regular payment amount: $120.00 Payment frequency: MONTHLY Amortization remaining: 168 months Year closing interest rate*: Royal Bank Prime + 1.000% = 5.500% per year

PRINCIPAL
Year opening principal balance: $14,684.59
Year closing principal balance: $14,027.90

INTEREST
Interest paid for reporting period: $743.37
Year opening interest rate: Royal Bank Prime + 1.000% = 5.000% per year

LoanProtector® Insurance:

PLEASE RETAIN THIS DOCUMENT FOR YOUR RECORDS.
THIS STATEMENT CAN BE USED FOR INCOME TAX PURPOSES.
ADDITIONAL COPIES WILL BE SUBJECT TO A NOMINAL FEE.

CREDIT LINE—AFTER

ROYAL BANK OF CANADA

RBC

ACCOUNT STATEMENT

ADEOLA OMOLE

Statement Date
31 May 2006

Re: Loan Account No.

Statement Period
2 May 2006 to 31 May 2006

Date	Description	Transaction Amount	Balance

Rate History

Your Interest Rate
ROYAL BK PRIME + 1.000 % = 7.000 %
History of Rates:
25 May - 31 May = 7.000 %
2 May - 24 May = 6.750 %

Credit Information

Credit limit:	17,000.00
Credit available at statement end date:	17,000.00

Account Information

Payment amount:	120.00
Payment due date:	22 Jun 2006
Past due payment:	N/A
Interest due date:	N/A
Accrued interest:	N/A

LoanProtector® Insurance:

New Royal Credit Line (RCL) account fees starting July 1, 2006
NSF fee of $35.00 for any RCL cheques that do not clear due to
insufficient available credit. Overlimit fee of $20.00 will be

charged each time your RCL is over your credit limit on the statement
date. These fees will be charged to your payment account.

ACCOUNT SUMMARY

Balance at 2 May 2006	Interest Paid	LoanProtector Insurance Paid	Withdrawals & Adjustments	Payments & Adjustments	Balance at 31 May 2006
.00 +	.00 +	.00 +	.00 +	.00 =	.00

If you notice any mistakes in your statement, you must let us know within 45 days of the statement date.

MBNA MASTERCARD—BEFORE

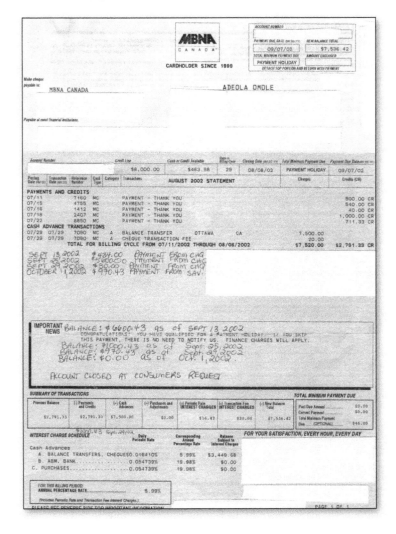

MBNA MASTERCARD—AFTER

MBNA
C A N A D A

ACCOUNT NUMBER	
PAYMENT DUE DATE mm dd yy	NEW BALANCE TOTAL
11/06/02	$16.88
TOTAL MINIMUM PAYMENT DUE	AMOUNT ENCLOSED
$10.00	$16.88

DETACH TOP PORTION AND RETURN WITH PAYMENT

Make cheque
payable to:

MBNA CANADA

ADEOLA OMOLE

Payable at most financial institutions.

Account Number		Credit Line	Cash or Credit Available	Days in Billing Cycle	Closing Date (mm/dd/yy)	Total Minimum Payment Due	Payment Due Date (mm/dd/yy)
		$6,000.00		29	10/09/02	$10.00	11/06/02

Posting Date (mm/dd)	Transaction Date (mm/dd)	Reference Number	Card Type	Category	Transactions	Charges	Credits (CR)
					OCTOBER 2002 STATEMENT		

PAYMENTS AND CREDITS

09/16		6986	MC		PAYMENT – THANK YOU		424.00 CR
09/25	09/25	1353	MC		PAYMENT – THANK YOU		5,600.00 CR
10/01		4550	MC		PAYMENT – THANK YOU		30.00 CR
10/03		3412	MC		PAYMENT – THANK YOU		870.43 CR
					TOTAL FOR BILLING CYCLE FROM 09/11/2002 THROUGH 10/09/2002	$0.00	$7,034.43 CR

IMPORTANT NEWS

OCTOBER 31, 2002 $16.88 Payment from chq   conf # 9386

BALANCE: 0.00

SUMMARY OF TRANSACTIONS

Previous Balance	(-) Payments and Credits	(-) Cash Advances	(+) Purchases and Adjustments	(+) Periodic Rate INTEREST CHARGES	(+) Transaction Fee INTEREST CHARGES	(=) New Balance Total
$7,034.43	$7,034.43	$0.00	$0.00	$16.88	$0.00	$16.88

TOTAL MINIMUM PAYMENT DUE

Past Due Amount	$0.00
Current Payment	$10.00
Total Minimum Payment Due	$10.00

INTEREST CHARGE SCHEDULE

	Daily Periodic Rate	Corresponding Annual Percentage Rate	Balance Subject to Interest Charges
Cash Advances			
A. BALANCE TRANSFERS, CHEQUES	0.016410%	5.99%	$3,547.20
B. ABM, BANK	0.057479%	20.98%	$0.00
C. PURCHASES	0.057479%	20.98%	$0.00

FOR THIS BILLING PERIOD: ANNUAL PERCENTAGE RATE	5.99%

(Includes Periodic Rate and Transaction Fee Interest Charges.)

FOR YOUR SATISFACTION, EVERY HOUR, EVERY DAY

PLEASE SEE REVERSE SIDE FOR IMPORTANT INFORMATION

PAGE 1 OF 1

CAPITAL ONE MASTERCARD–BEFORE

CapitalOne

GOLD MASTERCARD ACCOUNT   JAN 14 - FEB 13, 2002
                                            Page 1 of 1

Account Summary

Previous Balance	$7,582.06
Payments, Credits and Adjustments	$200.00
Transactions	$.00
Finance Charges	$74.28
New Balance	$7,456.34
Minimum Amount Due	$.00
Payment Due Date	March 08, 2002
Total Credit Line	$16,000
Total Available Credit	$8,543.66
Credit Line for Cash	$8,000
Available Credit for Cash	$7,967.67

At your service

To call Customer Relations or to report a lost or stolen card:
Canada and the United States 1-800-481-3239

Send payments to: Send enquiries to:

Payments, Credits and Adjustments

1	06 FEB	PAYMENT	$200.00-

February 28, 2002 $200.00 Pmt from savings
conf # J800w9
Balance: 7,256.34

Finance Charges

Please see reverse side for important information

	Balance rate applied to	Periodic rate	Corresponding APR	FINANCE CHARGE
PURCHASES	$2,976.79 N	1.49%	17.90%	$44.40
CASH	$53.25 N	1.49%	17.90%	$.48
SPECIAL TRANSFERS	$4,465.53 N	.66%	7.90%	$29.40

ANNUAL PERCENTAGE RATE applied this period   11.93%

10377

▼ PLEASE RETURN PORTION BELOW WITH PAYMENT. ▼

CapitalOne

0000000 0   00000000

New Balance	$7,456.34
Minimum Amount Due	$.00
Payment Due Date	March 08, 2002
Total enclosed	$ 200.7

Please print address changes below using blue or black ink.

Street		Apt #
City	Province	Postal Code
Home Phone	Alternate Phone	

ADEOLA OMOLE

$74.28 Interest Payment

CAPITAL ONE MASTERCARD—AFTER

Capital One	GOLD MASTERCARD ACCOUNT	MAR 14 - APR 13, 2002
		Page 1 of 1

Account Summary

Previous Balance	$7,329.08
Payments, Credits and Adjustments	$7,353.64
Transactions	$24.56
Finance Charges	$.00
New Balance	$0.00
Minimum Amount Due	$.00
Payment Due Date	May 09, 2002
Total Credit Line	$10,000
Total Available Credit	$10,000.00
Credit Line for Cash	$5,000
Available Credit for Cash	$5,000.00

At your service

To call Customer Relations or to report a lost or stolen card:
Canada and the United States 1-800-481-3239

Send payments to: Send inquiries to:

Payments, Credits and Adjustments

1	28 MAR	PAYMENT	$200.00
2	08 APR	PAYMENT	1,000.00
3	08 APR	PAYMENT	111.71
4	10 APR	PAYMENT	1,000.00
5	10 APR	PAYMENT	5,041.93

Transactions

6	12 MAR	AOL*CANADA SERVICE	$24.56

Finance Charges

Please see reverse side for important information

	Balance rate applied to	Periodic rate	Corresponding APR	FINANCE CHARGE
PURCHASES	$.00 N	.00%	.00%	$.00
CASH	$.00 N	.00%	.00%	$.00

ANNUAL PERCENTAGE RATE applied this period   0.00%

45194

▼ PLEASE RETURN PORTION BELOW WITH PAYMENT. ▼

Capital One

0000000 0   00000000 00000000

New Balance	$0.00
Minimum Amount Due	$.00
Payment Due Date	May 09, 2002
Total enclosed	$

Please print address changes below using blue or black ink.

Street	Apt #
City	Province
Home Phone	Alternate Phone

ACCOUNT HAS BEEN CLOSED   ADEOLA OMOLE

CITIBANK MASTERCARD—BEFORE

	0000		

Account Number	Total Balance	Payment Due Date
	5,361.50	12/05/2002

Payable at Most Financial Institutions*

Please check (✓) the box that applies:
☐ Minimum Payment 112.59
☐ Total Balance 5,361.50
☐ Other Amount $ ☐☐☐☐☐☐

ADEOLA OMOLE

CITIBANK CANADA

⑈900⑉   96

DETACH AND RETURN ABOVE PORTION WITH YOUR PAYMENT

citi

Citi Platinum MasterCard

Statement Date
11/15/2002

Payment Due Date
12/05/2002

Purchase Date	Reference Number	Description	Amount
10/29	88202303	CIBC	70.00-
10/31	88202305	CIBC	45.50-
11/04	88202309	CIBC	23.00-

Effective November 1, 2002, the carrier for your
travel accident insurance will be changed to Chubb
Insurance Company of Canada. Please refer to the
Description of Coverage form you will receive in
your December statement for complete details.

Remember, use your Citi MasterCard Card anywhere
between Nov. 1 - Dec. 31, 2002 for an automatic
chance to win 1 of 5 Grand Prize Get-together
Trips from MasterCard. You could take whomever you
want, wherever you want.

[handwritten] NOVEMBER 22, 2002 $400.00 PAYMENT FROM CHQ. REF# 7176 BALANCE 4961.5

Account Summary		Available Credit	
Previous Balance	5,500.00	Total Credit Limit	5,600
+New Purchases	0.00	Available Credit Limit	238
+Cash Advances	0.00	Amount Over Credit Limit	0.00
+Interest Charges	0.00	Total New Balance	5,361.50
-Payments and Credits	138.50	Amount Past Due	0.00
Total New Balance	5,361.50	Minimum Payment Due	112.59
		Amount Paid	(For your records)

Interest Charge Information

	Purch. effective 09/26/2002	Purch. effective 09/26/2002	Cash Advances
Balance Subject to Interest Charges	5,421.93	0.00	0.00
Annual Interest Rate	0.00%	17.90%	17.90%
Periodic Rate	0.00000%	1.49170%	0.04904%
(Purchases-Monthly, Advances-Daily)			

[handwritten] Last payment for o/s is March Statement Btwn March 5-10 2003

CITIBANK MASTERCARD—AFTER

Account Number	Total Balance	Payment Due Date
	0.00	04/10/2003

Please check (✓) the box that applies:

☐ Minimum Payment 0.00
☐ Total Balance 0.00
☐ Other Amount $

Payable at Most Financial Institutions*

ADEOLA OMOLE   4444   CITIBANK CANADA

"900" 96

citi
Citi Platinum MasterCard

DETACH AND RETURN ABOVE PORTION WITH YOUR PAYMENT.

Statement Date 03/18/2003
Account Number
Payment Due 04/10/2003

Purchase Date	Reference Number	Description	Amount
02/20	88203052	CIBC	335.00-
03/04	88203064	CIBC	3,997.33-
		With your Citi MasterCard card, access cash instantly at 835,000 ABM's worldwide. Just look for the Interac or Cirrus logo. Forgot your PIN? Call 1-800-387-1616 to request a new one or inquire about selecting your own.	

Previous Balance	4,332.33	Total Credit Limit	5,600
+New Purchases	0.00	Available Credit Limit	5,600
+Cash Advances	0.00	Amount Over Credit Limit	0.00
+Interest Charges	0.00	Total New Balance	0.00
-Payments and Credits	4,332.33	Amount Past Due	0.00
Total New Balance	0.00	Minimum Payment Due	0.00
		Amount Paid	(For your records)

Interest Charge Information

	Balance Subject to Interest Charges	Annual Interest Rate	Periodic Rate (must annu, adv. Daily)
Purchases	0.00	17.90%	1.49170%
Cash Advances	0.00	17.90%	0.04904%

1327

STUDENT LOAN #1—BEFORE

Royal Bank of Canada

DISCLOSURE STATEMENT

ADEOLA OMOLE

Statement Date	Loan Account No.
28 Sep 2001	-007

Loan Description   **Your Interest Rate per year**

VARIABLE RATE LOAN   ROYAL BK PRIME + 2.500 % = 7.750 %

Account Details

Term	N/A
Payment amount (including LoanProtector® Insurance Premium, if applicable)	154.00
Payment due date	1 Oct 2001
Amortization	114 MONTHS
Triggering Interest Rate	16.100 %
Annual Percentage Rate (if there are no cost of borrowing charges other than interest, then this will equal your interest rate)	7.750 %
Payment Frequency**	monthly

This statement has been produced to advise you of changes to your total Cost of Borrowing based on recent changes/amendments to your loan account.

COST OF BORROWING

Outstanding Loan Balance	Total Payments to the end of the term*	Total Cost of Borrowing* (If no Cost of Borrowing Charges then this amount identifies your total interest cost)
10,579.16	14,014.00	3,450.49
	*Based on current interest rate. If you have LoanProtector® insurance, please see reverse.	*Based on current interest rate. If you have LoanProtector® insurance, please see reverse.

◆ Royal Bank Prime Rate is the annual rate of interest announced from time to time by us as a reference rate then in effect for determining interest rates on Canadian dollar commercial loans in Canada.

STUDENT LOAN #1—AFTER

ROYAL BANK OF CANADA

RBC

Page 1 of 1

ADEOLA OMOLE

Statement Date
01 Dec 2004

Student Loan Annual Statement

Canada Student Loan
Account Number: 007

Transaction Summary		Interest Information	
Principal balance on 13 Mar 2004	7,544.96	Effective Rate	6.75 %
Payments to Principal	7,544.96	Prime	4.25 %
Current Principal Balance	0.00	Premium	2.50 %

Royal Bank appreciates the opportunity to serve all your banking needs.

STUDENT LOAN #2—BEFORE

Royal Bank of Canada

DISCLOSURE STATEMENT

ADEOLA OMOLE

Statement Date	**Loan Account No.**
28 Sep 2001	*r*-008

Loan Description	**Your Interest Rate per year**
VARIABLE RATE LOAN	ROYAL BK PRIME + 2.500 % = 7.750 %

Account Details

Term	N/A
Payment amount (including LoanProtector® Insurance Premium, if applicable)	71.00
Payment due date	1 Oct 2001
Amortization	112 MONTHS
Triggering Interest Rate	16.216 %
Annual Percentage Rate (if there are no cost of borrowing charges other than interest, then this will equal your interest rate)	7.750 %
Payment Frequency**	monthly

This statement has been produced to advise you of changes to your total Cost of Borrowing based on recent changes/amendments to your loan account.

COST OF BORROWING

Outstanding Loan Balance	Total Payments to the end of the term*	Total Cost of Borrowing* (If no Cost of Borrowing Charges then this amount identifies your total interest cost)
4,837.11	6,390.00	1,558.67
	*Based on current interest rate. If you have LoanProtector® insurance, please see reverse.	*Based on current interest rate. If you have LoanProtector® Insurance, please see reverse.

❖ Royal Bank Prime Rate is the annual rate of interest announced from time to time by us as a reference rate then in effect for determining interest rates on Canadian dollar commercial loans in Canada.

STUDENT LOAN #2—AFTER

ROYAL BANK OF CANADA

RBC

Page 1 of 1

ADEOLA OMOLE

Statement Date
01 Nov 2004

Student Loan Annual Statement

Alberta Student Loan
Account Number   008

Transaction Summary		Interest Information	
Principal balance on 13 Mar 2004	3,430.62	Effective Rate	6.75 %
Payments to Principal	3,430.62	Prime	4.25 %
Current Principal Balance	0.00	Premium	2.50 %

Royal Bank appreciates the opportunity to serve all your banking needs.

OVERDRAWN VISA

ROYAL BANK · **VISA** GOLD · *No Fee Now. No Fee Later.*

ADEOLA OMOLE

Previous Balance	Purchases & Debits	Cash Advances	Interest & Fees	Payments & Credits	NEW BALANCE
5,129.99	0.00	219.00	46.51	155.00	5,240.50

Transaction Date	Transaction Description	Amount (CR = Credit)	✓
AUG 18	PAYMENT - THANK YOU / PAIEMENT - MERCI	155.00 (CR)	
SEP 02	TELBANK CASH ADV/AVANCE DE FONDS -1004	219.00	
SEP 04	CASH ADVANCE INTEREST	1.88	
SEP 04	PURCHASE INTEREST	44.63	

TO AVOID INTEREST CHARGES ON NEW PURCHASES, YOU MUST MAKE A PAYMENT OF AT LEAST THE AMOUNT OF YOUR "NEW BALANCE" BY THE "DUE DATE" SHOWN ON THIS STATEMENT.

YOUR CREDIT LIMIT HAS BEEN EXCEEDED. PLEASE ENSURE YOUR PAYMENT INCLUDES THE OVERLIMIT AMOUNT OUTSTANDING AS WELL AS THE MINIMUM PAYMENT DUE.

PAY WITH YOUR VISA CARD AT PARTICIPATING PIZZA HUT DINE-IN RESTAURANTS IN CANADA FROM AUGUST 13TH - SEPTEMBER 23RD, 2001 AND YOU COULD ENTER TO WIN A FAMILY CRUISE VACATION FOR 4.... OR WIN THOUSANDS OF INSTANT PRIZES! EVERY GAME CARD WINS INSTANTLY! FOR MORE DETAILS VISIT A PARTICIPATING PIZZA HUT NEAR YOU.

Credit Limit	Available Credit	Statement Date	DUE DATE	Past Due	Minimum Payment	Amount Paid
5,000	0	SEP 04/01	SEP 21/01	0.00	158.00	$ 219

PAGE 1 OF 1

TRANSACTION TYPE	Interest Rate
Interest-Bearing Purchases	10.50 %
Cash Advances and Cheques	10.50 %

ROYAL BANK VISA
PAYMENT CENTRE

Payment Due Date	New Balance	Minimum Payment	Amount Paid
SEP 21/01	5,240.50	158.00	$ 219

CARD NUMBER:

Payment Options:

ADEOLA OMOLE

96

OVERDRAWN CHEQUING ACCOUNT

As you can see, although I had a lot of debt, I was able to take the necessary steps to pay off each debt, and I'm confident that you will be able to take the steps required to pay off your debt too. I truly do hope that sharing the before and after snapshot of my debt has helped you on your own personal debt free journey. Remember, each payment you make towards your debt will lead you closer to the creation of abundant wealth in your life. Go out there and claim your wealth!

ACKNOWLEDGMENTS

There are a number of people whom I want to thank. First and foremost, I want to thank my amazing husband, Adam, for always believing in me, and for being my number one supporter. From the moment I announced that I had created a strategy to get us out of debt, to the moment that I announced that I was writing a book to share this strategy with the world, he has been there for me throughout this journey, with his invisible pompoms cheering me on. I also want to thank my two incredible kids for giving me the time that I needed to write this book, and for never complaining when I had to spend time away from them to write the book.

I am so deeply grateful for the support of my sister and brother-in-law, Bisi and Dave Read. They were both instrumental in helping me with very important details required for the book, such as proofreading my manuscript, providing invaluable feedback on the overall content of the book, and also lending guidance on the book cover design. Thank you both so much!

I humbly acknowledge both Derek Foster and Sean Cooper, my fellow writers, who generously took time out of their busy lives to read my manuscript, and provide me with invaluable information and guidance on the book publishing and marketing process.

I am grateful to David Jupijn for giving me an incredible opportunity to share my story with his podcast listeners. But more importantly, I feel blessed to have met him, and deeply grateful for his enthusiastic support of my book.

Finally, I want to thank Bola Sokunbi, the founder of Clever Girl Finance, for inviting me to be a guest on her podcast, and giving me an opportunity to share my story with her incredible audience of women. Thank you for allowing me to impact the lives of so many wonderful women who are striving to improve their financial lives.

ABOUT THE AUTHOR

Adeola Omole lives in the beautiful Rocky Mountains of Canada with her wonderful husband and two incredible children. A life altering financial setback in her late twenties resulted in her being out of work for eighteen months. This experience motivated her to create a two part financial strategy that resulted in her paying off over $390,000 of debt, and allowed her to reach millionaire status in her thirties. She successfully grew her 7-figure net worth by investing in real estate, the stock markets, her business, and herself. She spends her days caring for her children, while running her wealth coaching business. Adeola is a lawyer by training, but has made it her life's mission to teach other's how to get out of debt, stay out of debt, and build life changing wealth. She is living her life's passion, and is grateful to have the opportunity to impact and transform the lives of so many people.

CPSIA information can be obtained
at www.ICGtesting.com
Printed in the USA
LVHW03s1433111018
593271LV00013B/1108/P